Dhairyapath

AN AUTOBIOGRAPHY

Dhairyapath

AN AUTOBIOGRAPHY

JITENDER JOSHI

Translated by
Dr. Kumar Shravan

PRABHAT
PRAKASHAN

Published by
PRABHAT PRAKASHAN PVT. LTD.
4/19 Asaf Ali Road,
New Delhi-110 002 (INDIA)
e-mail: prabhatbooks@gmail.com

ISBN 978-93-5562-080-4
DHAIRYAPATH: AN AUTOBIOGRAPHY
by Jitender Joshi

Edition
First, 2024

Price
₹ 750 (Rupees Seven Hundred Fifty Only)

Printed at
Japan Art, Delhi

A Few Memories

Dedicated to my respected parents

Late Pt Shri Sureshanand Joshi and Late Smt. Sushila Devi

प्रदोषे दीपकः चंद्रः, प्रभाते दीपकः रविः

त्रैलोक्ये दीपकः धर्मः, सुपुत्रः कुलदीपकः ।।

–**Subhashitam 6**

pradoshe deepakah chandrah, prabhate deepakah ravi
trailokye deepakah dharmah, suputrah kuldeepakah

(The moon illuminates the evening, the sun illuminates the morning, dharma illuminates all the three worlds and a capable son illuminates all ancestors.)

Lt Gen. Gurmit Singh
PVSM, UYSM, AVSM, VSM
(Retd)

Governor of Uttarakhand

Rajbhawan Uttarakhand
Dehradun-248003
Phone : 0135-2757400
2757403

06.05.2023

सत्यमेव जयते

Message

I am very pleased to know that Shri Jitender Joshi, Chancellor of Uttaranchal University, has penned an autobiography based on his life journey. He has, in his autobiography, expressed his thoughts on the struggles and achievements in his life.

Even before the publication of this autobiography based on his life journey, Shri Joshi Ji had sent me some pages of the same reminding me that it was the after-effects of the inspiration he got from me; this made me quite happy. This, in my view, is an inspirational book, as it depicts struggles fructifying into achievements, ideas taking shape and an ordinary individual attaining the glory of an extraordinary.

I hope, rather I am confident that this story of struggles would definitely awaken the finest emotions inside the reader to turn the impossible into the possible; at the same time, this would also work as a great inspiration for the youth.

I send my compliments and best wishes for the publication of this autobiography.

गुरमीत

–Lt Gen. Gurmit Singh
PVSM, UYSM, AVSM, VSM (Retd)

Pushkar Singh Dhami

मुख्यमंत्री उत्तराखंड

Uttarakhand Secretariat
Dehradun-248001
Secretariat Phone: 0135-2716262
0135-2650433
Fax: 0135-2712827
Assembly Phone: 0135-2665100
0135-2665497
Fax: 0135-2666166
Email : cm-ua@nic.in

Message

I am extremely happy to learn that Shri Jitender Joshi Ji, founder Chancellor of Uttaranchal University, one of the leading educational institutions of the state, is bringing out his autobiography. Shri Joshi Ji has carried out several commendable jobs in the field of education, including the establishment of a law institute, securing NAAC A+ accreditation for the university and several initiatives for the benefit of farmers on the hills, facilitating better education as well as self-employment for the people there. I hope Joshi Ji is going to share his experiences relating to all those commendable initiatives taken by him in the field of education for the benefit of society; they would undoubtedly prove to be very inspirational for the coming generations.

I send my heartiest congratulations and best wishes to Shri Jitender Joshi Ji for the successful publication of his autobiography. *Dhairyapath An autobiography*.

–Pushkar Singh Dhami

Dr Hariom Panwar

एल.एल.एम. एल.एल.डी.
अध्यक्ष-पँवार वाणी फाउंडेशन, मेरठ
पूर्व डीन-विधि संकल्प-चौधरी चरण सिंह विश्वविद्यालय, मेरठ
पूर्व अध्यक्ष-कानून विभाग, मेरठ कॉलेज, मेरठ
पूर्व संयोजन-बोर्ड ऑफ स्टडीज कानून विभाग
चौ. चरण सिंह विश्वविद्यालय, मेरठ

Message

I had the opportunity to go through a few pages of the manuscript of the autobiography written by dear Shri Jitender Joshi Ji whom I hold in high regard; those few pages provided me a perspective of his work life and his resolve, his decisions and his inspirational works.

The script also made me realise that not only a stream of thoughts keeps flowing in the mind of Shri Joshi Ji who usually remains calmly engrossed in his work, but he also has a penchant for chiselling those thoughts, turning them into resolve and finally giving them shape after bringing them to a decisive state.

When a person's life starts taking shape after going through various struggles and when those struggles culminate in a pleasant result, he feels real happiness and contentment.

In his autobiography, he has described in detail how he gave his casual hobby of gardening such a massive shape while also attending to all his daily routines and discharging all his responsibilities appropriately.

In the form of this book, he has presented a great and exemplary piece for all of us and the coming generations.

Society must be witnessed to such work that could be a source of inspiration in the times to come.

Whenever thoughts are turned into resolve in life, and attempts are made to materialise them with a positive approach, nothing stands in the way of making them possible.

This is the hidden spirit and the core point of the entire endeavour of Shri Joshi Ji. Shri Joshi Ji usually says, "You should do your work with the same edification that you often give to others." This is a great thought of life.

In his autobiography, he has written, "The goal of life is to have a life full of goals."

I also believe that a person's life may be considered successful only when he either writes something that is read or commented on by others in the times to come or he does something that becomes a model necessary to be followed or written about in the future. From this point of view, Shri Jitender Joshi has executed his jobs in both forms with great finesse.

I heartily congratulate Joshi Ji for this publication and wish him great success in his life. With the best of compliments,

–Dr Hariom Panwar

Author's Note

Now, the book is complete, and this is the last task related to the book.

Well, how about a story for now? I will tell you something later as it comes to my mind.

Once, a rishi (the teacher) was teaching his students in a gurukul when suddenly something came to his mind. He asked a student sitting in the first row to pick up a basket of guavas lying beside him and distribute one guava each to every student. The rishi then said, "I am going outside for a while; keep the guavas safe until I return." The rishi then went out.

He returned after around two hours and asked the students about their guavas. There were only two students who had followed the rishi's instruction; they had not eaten their guavas. He gave each of them a basket full of guavas. All the other students were surprised. They were not able to understand why their teacher had done so. The rishi then explained to the students. He said, "I knew you all were hungry right from the morning. Still, I gave each of you one guava and asked you not to eat the same until I returned. This was a test of your patience. Only two of you could pass the same; the rest of you could not control your hunger. These baskets full of guavas are rewards for their patience." He further said, "We fail to be patient in our life and hence get deprived of something great in life. Hence, we should always have patience. Efforts many a time seek patience."

How was the story? I heard this story in my childhood and in every situation, this story has reminded me to have patience.

In this Author's Note, I have to say that I am still unable to believe that all the memories of my journey in life have been penned on paper and taken the shape of a book. I would hear a lot... this autobiography... that autobiography. Ultimately, all those words made me give shape to my own autobiography. My thanks to destiny that inspired me to write. Otherwise, where did I have the time to spare from my busy schedule so that I could sit down with pen and paper and write my autobiography? And as this book is in your hands, many thanks to you for showing interest in going through the same.

Only while writing this, I realise how difficult it was to write about oneself.

What's there to hide? I am not highly educated... but I never allowed my morale to sink while facing difficult situations. I never dreamt small. My entire journey, from selling milk to establishing a university, has been a test of my courage and patience. I did fall at times... but have also risen after that, and that's what this autobiography has chronicled in all its pages.

If this journey of mine turns out to be an inspiration for you in any way, the autobiography would be a real success. And that is its purpose.

Contents

1

My Childhood

For a moment, I was a bit overwhelmed as I gazed at the tree leaves fluttering in the breeze. They appeared to be cooling the sun's heat by filtering the rays. Ponder over it. It seems to be a remarkable phenomenon, isn't it? How beautifully the rays from the sun, whose heat makes us uncomfortable, are cooled down by some leaves and dispersed over the ground, akin the blinking stars!

Life is probably somewhat similar. It is always surrounded by the heat of problems and challenges. Some people can confront these challenges like the tree and turn them into opportunities, while others succumb to them.

I am not saying this to liken myself to the tree. It's just a life statement for me, and hence I have started with the same. Moreover, an autobiography is never a means to portray oneself as a hero; rather, it's a means for self-exploration. It's up to people to make their own judgements about the same. I have just started to write...

By the time this book reaches you, I will have completed a 62-year journey of my life.

Writing an autobiography was not my idea. I don't see myself as a writer eager to showcase writing skills in this genre, nor have I ever thought of myself as someone with a story worthy of being penned. Much like everyone else, I've faced my fair share of life's struggles. What makes my experiences worth writing about?

If I may speak a somewhat deeper truth, life, in fact, never provided an opportunity to have some time to reflect on myself and think in that direction. I always remained bogged down—sometimes with paucity, sometimes in struggles, and then in the fight to attain my dreams.

This stage of my life brought me in contact with some people who encouraged me to dream big. It involves an intriguing tale—the story of an apple—that laid the foundation for this autobiography. When we typically think of an apple, the first thing that comes to mind is Newton's Law of Gravitation. However, in the context of my autobiography, the apple provides a testimony to the victory over the attraction and challenges of relationships.

It might not immediately resonate with you, so let me elucidate.

During a formal meeting with the Honourable Governor of Uttarakhand, I extended my congratulations on his new role and presented him with a basket of apples from my orchards, accompanied by a bouquet. The Governor, surprised, looked at me and inquired, "Are you involved in apple farming?" With a smile, I nodded and shared the narrative of my journey in apple farming. After hearing the highs and lows of my story, he remarked, “This must be documented. It could serve as a truly inspiring tale for people.”

The formalities concluded, and I left the Raj Bhavan. Despite appearing calm in the car, my mind buzzed with restlessness. Upon deeper reflection, I could figure out that it was nothing but the Honourable Governor’s suggestion that my story should be penned that had been making my mind restive. That was the moment when the seed of writing dropped into the soil of my mind and asserted its insistence on germination.

Back from the meeting, I was sitting alone in my office. There was a dim light in a corner of the office. I could hear the chirps of a squirrel coming through the window. Suddenly, my eyes started roaming over my past achievements displayed on the office walls. Every single picture appeared to be telling its own story, urging me to write about them. When my gaze moved away from the pictures, it settled on the apples kept in a tray at the corner of the table. I picked up an apple and holding it in my hand, like a parent cradles their child. Words fall short in capturing the emotions I felt while cradling the apple in my hand that day.

All the scenes of my journey to date started coming out of some darkness and appearing before me crystal clear as if that seed had suddenly dug all of them out—akin to flashbacks in films.

I took a deep breath and looked towards the window where a squirrel darted between branches. While watching that, suddenly, a rough and rocky lane appeared before me. I saw a mountain boy swinging his bag and running down the rocky path barefoot.

Was that boy me? The answer resonated—Yes, Jitender, that boy is you! That is you—the beloved barrister of his mother! And that is the beginning of your journey!

I had found the beginning! I resolved to write—my autobiography, chronicling my pain and suffering from that walk, right from the beginning.

I retrieved a diary from my cupboard and started writing whatever I was feeling at that moment.

That day, I felt inspired yet somewhat uncertain. It seemed as if my childhood held my hand while I wrote. I was writing but my attention was repeatedly drawn towards my hand that was busy writing.

I remember, even before that, I would many a time keep looking at my hands for no specific reason and try to observe my fine hairs on the same. I would enjoy that. That day, the hair were visible quite clearly.

Transported back in time—some 50 years prior—I had just crossed the first decade of my age. I was feeling happy for some reason. I am just not able to recollect what that matter was. However, whenever I try to recollect that feeling, the excitement of my childhood appears to be getting fresh. I still remember how I would, when I was a kid, keep humming songs, the words of which would not even make sense. And why not? When does childhood get bogged down in meanings? Once mired in meaning, it ceases to be childhood.

I can't recall from where I learnt it, but whenever I encountered water, I would take some paper, make a boat and let it float on the water. Games such as *Gilli-danda, kancha-goli,* and sling, though seldom played today, were my cherished sources of joy. I wasn't known for academic pursuits, instead I excelled as an adept player in these traditional games..

The hills were my companions, then and now. Even today, I derive pleasure from watching the sun, its redness rising behind the towering hills. The distinction lies in the fact that, back then, I imagined the sun residing somewhere just beyond those lofty hills. Now, I comprehend its home and understand its struggles. Its journey, from rise to setting, inspires us to stay focused on our pursuits and serves as an example that, regardless of circumstances, one should continue moving forward.

I know very well what slogging and struggling mean, as my childhood diary had, besides the fascinating stories, reflected the challenges of scarcity.

As you must have gathered, I come from a hilly region. It's commonly said that people tend to grow weary after an extended stay in one place. However, people from the hills never grow bored of their surroundings. They consistently yearn to stay there and make these landscapes their permanent abode.

The rocky path of our village is the same even today.

I was born in Syalsi village of Jaunpur block

in Tehri Garhwal district of Uttarakhand. However, my roots trace back to Pokhra village in the Pauri Garhwal district.

If you are not acquainted with hilly villages, the term "backward village" might evoke an image of a road cutting through the middle of the village. But, just make a trip to a village in the hills, and you'll discover that many are still inaccessible by roads. Getting to these villages becomes a strenuous task, taxing on your feet. My village even today lacks the convenience of a proper road. Describing the challenges we faced during that time is difficult to express in words, but I'll illustrate with pictures and share my experiences as I begin writing this autobiography.

We are four brothers and four sisters. My father, Pt Sureshanand Joshi Ji, worked in the Postal Department. My mother's name is Smt. Sushila Devi. The university today is managed by a society named after her. Our mother instilled moral lessons in us, always enveloping each of her children in her love and affection. She encouraged us not to shy away from challenges but to face them fearlessly. This lesson has proven invaluable in my life journey to date. My mother used to say that we are Pahari people, and as Paharis, we must have sturdy legs and lungs. It is rightly said that a mother is one who can take the place of all others but whose place no one else can take.

Our home was always buzzing with activities; and everyone was in a joyous mood. We were a simple family, relying solely on my father's salary as the only source of income. If there was ever any kind of dearth, we never felt it. This was the result of the art of living that we had imbibed from our parents, and I received an ample share of love from my elder brothers and sisters. My mother would often share an incident. During my elder sister's send-off after her marriage, she began crying in our father's arms. I couldn't bear it; I grabbed my sister and started crying too. I shouted loudly, "Nobody should take my sister away." Not only that, when her in-laws tried to convince me, I even picked up stones to hit them.

Now whenever I recollect the incident, I can't help but laugh, and my siblings often bring it up just to tease me. Despite our differing dreams, one thing was common among us—we understood our domestic situation and responsibilities well. Deprivation never overwhelmed us; instead we always got together to face it happily.

As I mentioned earlier, my father worked in the Postal Department and was transferred at regular intervals. He started his job in Mussoorie, and after multiple transfers, completed his tenure at FRI (Forest Research Institute), Dehradun. His transfers always entailed the relocation of the entire family, resulting in changes in our schools each time.

Our school was around 3-4 kilometers away from our house. In the hills, distances are usually long. We always remembered our mother's words: "*Paharis* should have strong legs and lungs." These words kept us encouraged, tirelessly fueling our spirits and warding off any sense of fatigue.

I recall it was quite a difficult road. Just imagine what the condition would have been then if even today, we find the same kind of roads there. But we had learned to live in whatever circumstances we were in, and every good or bad time in our life provided us with something to learn.

Not only going to school but even buying things was quite difficult. We had to go to Mussoorie for the same, which was surely not less than 20 km away—some 15 km from Thatyur to Suwakholi and then a further 7 km to Mussoorie.

My mother was always concerned about our future. She wanted her sons to be responsible and independent.

I still remember we used to go to play, sneaking off without letting our mother know or by making some random excuse. Many a times, we would be rewarded with a good thrashing for such misdemeanours. There was a canal just next to our school, and I would often jump into it, catch some waterfowl and take them home. However, my mother was dead against that. She would never inflict harm on anyone, nor harbor any desire to cause harm.

She would say that we should not take away anybody's freedom, freeing all the waterfowl. Compared to our mother, our father was quite lenient. One disciplinarian in the family was enough.

My mother possessed a keen sense of attentiveness. She would listen to us very carefully and then lovingly explain things. We, the siblings, inherited this trait from her. Personally, I follow a similar approach in my professional life—I consult my colleagues, engage in discussions to thoroughly understand issues, and only then make decisions. I believe this is a fundamental management trait.

Anyway, I am casually referring to these things. In fact, setbacks were a familiar part of our lives, and we never viewed them as problems. The towering hills didn't intimidate us; we found joy in their ups and downs. Along the lanes to and from school, we honed our skills in games like *gilli-danda*, *kancha-goli* and sling.

Our childhood swiftly passed during our seven years in Thapla. I want to highlight that today's children often complain despite enjoying abundant comfort and amenities. True knowledge acquisition involves a form of disciplined practice, or sadhana, which is sometimes affected by the means available.

I'm not suggesting one shouldn't utilize means and amenities; rather, they should be leveraged. However, it's crucial to recognize that privation is a part of life, and often, facing such challenges can lead to achieving great success, as privation holds its own sentiments.

I don't mean to praise myself, but I want to convey that I viewed every privation as an opportunity. I sought possibilities in every situation, a practice I continue to uphold. Through hard work, I've fulfilled every need. My siblings and I never complained about the lack of amenities in our house; we lived happily even without ample means and facilities.

It seems like I've written quite a bit today, and I had almost lost myself in the narrative. Now, a new chapter is about to unfold in my life. I'll share that in the next installment. The beginning of my family journey directed me to where I stand today. How did it all happen? Well, I'll delve into that in the next chapter. As you explore your dreams, let's meet again tomorrow.

With memories of my childhood home

❑

2

Family and Responsibilities

Have you ever listened to the quietness of dawn? It's curious that people say silence doesn't make a sound. Perhaps one needs to transform the world within to truly hear that subtle sound. The mind can perceive every nuance of what is silent to the world. I often find solace in this quietude, like a blank canvas where I can imprint my thoughts and dreams. Memories are vivid, and now, I've arrived at precisely the point where I left off.

My mother always laid emphasis on the value of education for the young minds. While my brothers and sisters followed this dictum, I, however, did not delve deeply into my studies. I won't elaborate on the reasons; I leave it to you to discern as you journey through this chapter.

Time passed gradually. In 1972, my two elder brothers—Dinesh Bhaiji and Devendra Bhaiji—left to study at Ghananand Inter College in Mussoorie. I was just 10 years old then. After my elder brothers left home to study, regardless of my age, I became the eldest at home. Often, responsibility has a way of accelerating maturity beyond one's years.

After some time, my father was transferred from Thapla to Kalsi Post Office. We shifted to a rented house in Vikas Nagar, finding the place quite pleasant. I made many friends in the neighborhood, and we stayed there for a long time.

My siblings and I enrolled to Asharam Vedic Inter College situated around five kilometers from our residence in Vikas Nagar. We were a group of boys in the neighbourhood who would leave our houses at the same time and walk to school on foot every day. Reflecting on those times, a particular incident comes to mind. Once, while returning from school, my friends challenged me to use my sling to break the windscreen of the bus approaching us on the road. Who could stop me then? I picked up a stone, armed my sling, and closing one of my eyes, aimed the same at the target. The stone hit the car and broke its windscreen; Though I skillfully eluded the scene, the repercussions awaited me at home, where my mother's scolding reverberated through the walls. Yet, in the hallowed halls of the school, I stood adorned with a hero's laurels! Ha ha ha!

It gives me a different feeling when I recollect the incident now. It’s all memories now. Where is the option to tamper with the time or relive our memories? Let’s move ahead…

Now comes the turning point, which I consider a significant milestone, especially when I reflect on it from today's perspective. This moment marks an incident that, in my perspective, laid the cornerstone of my present self.

It's a stark reality that within the folds of adversity, seeds of something profoundly good can sprout. God, in his wisdom, orchestrates circumstances, be they easy or challenging, all for our ultimate benefit. Undoubtedly, such situations can be difficult, yet we must find ways to fortify ourselves for the trials and embrace every challenge as we forge ahead.

Before moving to Vikas Nagar, we had a cow and a buffalo at our house to meet our requirements for milk. When my father was transferred, we brought them with us to Vikas Nagar, having grown attached to them. Even today, I remember those gentle creatures fondly. However, the landlord of the house where we were staying in Vikas Nagar objected to keeping them there. We felt badly humiliated by his behaviour. The landlord stopped at nothing to lambast us. My parents, my sisters and I had to listen to all his nonsense mutely. He grumbled more probably because we had started selling surplus milk for additional income. The entire family contributed to the care of our livestock—my mother milking them, and I transporting the milk to Vikas Nagar in a can on my way to school. After selling the milk, I'd carry the empty can back on my return in the evening. This routine seemingly irked him, although other neighbors had similar arrangements. Nevertheless...

When you are poor and deprived, very few people give importance to you. I understood it then and resolved not to depend on anybody when I grew up; I would carve out my fate on my own. Although control over circumstances was limited at that time, there was a noticeable change happening within me.

One day, as my parents came inside the house after listening to all the harsh and unpalatable words, my mother said to my father, "I am unable to spend even a moment in this house now. Please do something. I don't want to stay here. Haven't we suffered enough humiliation? Are we going to leave only after he throws our stuff out of the house?"

My father was embarrassed and helpless that day. At the same time, I also observed some kind of courage in him. As I told you earlier, something bad brings something very good too with it. This humiliation provided a new direction to our family. After some time, my father took a bold decision and built a two-room house—half mud and half concrete—on the plot he had bought earlier in Etanbagh village of Herbertpur, not very far from our current residence.

House located in Etanbagh village of Herbertpur, in 2023.

We were finally free, owners of a small yet significant house on our own land. We re-initiated our milk business on a much larger scale.

This small work taught me many mantras of business—how to behave properly, how to be perfect in accounts and how to honor one's commitments. I had still not grown beyond my age, but I am able to recollect that all these ideas would instinctively keep floating in my mind—if I were well-behaved, I would attract customers. If I were accurate in my records, I would be able to understand profit-loss in business and if I were a man of my word, customers would be loyal to me. This job of a few litres of milk helped me develop an ocean of self-confidence for business.

After two to three years of involvement in the milk business a restless desire to do something more began to take hold. With time, our household expenses were also growing. My mind would be always restless to invest myself in new endeavors, though the exact path eluded me.

Then, suddenly, one day, an idea clicked in my mind. There was one work that had attracted my attention repeatedly. I felt I could manage that. I was a youth of this new age where every new dream could take flight instantly.

I came to know about the work related to the powder used for making *agarbattis*. I had seen this being managed by Shri Ravindra Jain of Herbertpur. His work was flourishing well at that time. Getting inspiration from him and with God's blessings, we installed a small factory in 1980 for the same; it was named 'Joshi & Company'. Let me explain the work involved in the process. You must be aware of *agarbattis*. The paste that was rolled around the sticks was made using pinewood powder and camphor powder. The same paste was also used to make *dhoop*. Our job was to prepare that powder using a pulveriser machine, pack them properly and send the same to factories producing *agarbattis*. Given the demand for agarbattis and dhoop, our powder also found significant traction. Blessed with abundant trees in our vicinity, we ventured forth.

However, launching the factory presented a challenge. My father, concerned about the uncertainties of business, wished for me to continue my studies and pursue a conventional job. He was not too happy to see my new interest. Every father wants to secure the future of his children, and he was concerned about me because of the ups and downs of the business. Even the milk business didn't have his absolute approval. It was my mother who was managing everything. As such, my mother and all my siblings always stood behind me for such ventures. It was like even if I said that I wanted to be Prime Minister of the country, they would not hesitate for a moment and come forward to support me and do everything that could help me attain my dream.

So, the main issue was convincing my father and to get his approval for the venture. One evening, armed with the support of my mother, I mustered the courage to tell my father that I wanted to start a new venture—for making pinewood powder. I explained to him that it was a flourishing business. I only had to buy and install a machine. My father said, "Go ahead. Have I ever stopped you for anything?"

I knew this was not an indication of his approval, and my presumption was correct. He further said, "Start but don't use our land. This land is not meant for such things. Find an alternate place and do it on your own." And then he left after reciting the following lines that I remember even today.

leek-leek gadi chale, leek hi chale kapoot
leek chhod teeno chale, shayar, singh, sapoot

(Just as vehicles trace the grooves of roads,
An unworthy son adheres to ready-made molds.
Contrarily, a poet, a lion, and a worthy son,
Forge paths uniquely, where their spirits run.)

I decided to go ahead with my plan. But there was still a problem—where to get funds for the project? Again an idea clicked in my mind. I told my mother about the requirement of money to buy the pulveriser machine and the machine to make packets. She took whatever she had saved out of the income from selling milk and handing over the same to me, said, "Go, Jitu, do something that may inspire others to follow."

My journey had covered a considerable distance by this point; I was 22 when it all began. In a short span, the project gained momentum, demanding much of my time. Balancing work and personal life became a struggle, but amid the challenges, I found contentment.

With the memories of my closed factory of Joshi & Co.

I would like to say something here. I never thought of shortcuts for success. This is the culture I have inherited from my family. I have always believed in my hard work.

I had to discontinue my studies after intermediate. I got busy with this very venture. I was finding my happiness and my expertise in this. I had the stamina to work the whole day—without stopping, without getting tired! Where was I going—I never thought of that. Just keep moving ahead—that's what I had resolved.

At this point, I would like to express my gratitude to my elder brother Shri Devendra Joshi Ji, who, working in the Irrigation Department in Dehradun, attempted to assist me in completing my studies. However, destiny had different plans, and the separation from my mother made it difficult for me to stay alone in Dehradun. Hence, I left everything and came back to my parents. As such, my brother, though alone, tried his best to provide me the love of a mother and the protection of a father, but I probably had to write my own destiny.

Everything looked to be going smoothly, but for one aspect. I was not able to spend much time with my mother. I learnt sometime later that my mother was not keeping well. Initially, I could not pay attention to the same and she also never told me about it. She was suffering from a breathing problem. Despite treatment and the best care, she did not live long.

One day, she suddenly left us alone. I felt as if I had lost everything. Every turn of my life was full of my mother's love, affection and fondness. She was an inspiration for all of us. Sadly, destiny has its own ways. For me, that was the most painful day. My mother would always teach morality. She would always enjoin us to be honest.

Now, apart from some pictures, only her messages are left with us.

As time passed, my two brothers and three sisters got married, and the memories of my mother somewhat dulled my senses. Expressing the pain of separation from one's mother is challenging, and even my pen seems hesitant to capture these emotions in words.

Okay then, let's reconvene in the next chapter with more memories.

❑

3

Will Not Accept Defeat

I'm not sure whether you'd agree with me, but I genuinely believe that in everything you do, there will always be something that gets overlooked. I say this based on my past experiences.

I never fretted too much about missing things in life because nothing is permanent. However, sometimes, even your wisdom fails you, and the loss of something becomes unbearable. For me, losing my mother was something like that. Without my mother, I doubt I could have summoned the courage to embark on any new venture. We usually consider a mother's caress as a means of expressing love, but that turns out to be your greatest strength. You might have noticed that a cow starts caressing her calf right from the moment it takes birth and the calf finally gets the strength to stand on its legs. Mother is that *Shakti*. I lost my mother when I was just 24. She left me when everything appeared to be going right. It had come to my mind many a time to make my mother's life more pleasant and comfortable. But then, you don't have control over everything!

I have just recollected something my mother had told me a few hours before leaving for her heavenly abode. I was sitting beside her. She was clutching one of my thumbs feebly with her weak fingers. She told me, "*Beta*! I don't know how long I am going to survive. But if I am not there, you must marry before my *barsi*. God is always with you. Things are going well...and will be fine in the future too. Hence, don't delay it. If you have love and respect for me, please do this for me."

Ma, I always wished you stayed with us forever. Everything would have been done in your presence and as per your wish ...but...

Anyway, my mother had already left...

Life does not allow us to stop, even when the weight of loss presses upon our hearts. It keeps presenting upcoming duties and responsibilities while the past gradually fades away.

Oh yes, one more point is coming to my mind. I used to keep roaming around... talking to people, and keeping in touch with them, as I had many friends and acquaintances there. And hence, my mother would casually call me 'Barrister'. I had never thought that this nickname would later turn out to be an inspiration for some great work. What was that work? How did I do that? I will tell you everything in detail...a little later...I will remind you.

For now, turning to Joshi & Company, where, as I recall, orders from agarbatti companies consistently poured in. I had also put in all my efforts for the same. I cared neither for my meals nor for timely sleep. I would however advice everyone to maintain a good routine for meals and sleep. Timely meals and timely sleep are very important. It was my mistake that I didn't realise the same at that age. You should learn and make amends if necessary.

One day, my father told me, "Jitender, now you should also marry. Let me fulfil the responsibility that your mother had assigned to me. I also wish the same."

My mother had perhaps told my father the same thing. But, how to find a suitable girl? Some proposals did come but none of them clicked. And now, let me tell you how I happened to meet Anuradha, my wife.

I used to be away from home on business trips for almost 15-20 days every month. And whenever I returned, I would find my father quite dejected. He would say that he was finding it difficult to stay alone at home.

I arranged for a Punditji as a sewak at home for cooking and taking care of my father. But still, whenever I returned from a business trip, I would have to listen to the same bitter words. I was focusing on growing my business, but the dejected look on my father's face ultimately compelled me to give my consent.

As mentioned earlier, my father was persistently after me to somehow get me married, and where there is a will, there is a way.

One day, Narendra Bishtji, a PTI at Asharam Vedic College where I had studied, happened to meet my father. Expressing his concerns, my father confided in him, and Bishtji, armed with a long list, promptly presented 5-6 marriage proposals, one of which was for Anuradha. She, too, belonged to a Brahmin family, mirroring our own background. I am not aware of what transpired between my father and Bishtji. He just gave me instructions one day that I needed to go to Dehradun and meet the girl's father.

Had it been an instruction to meet the girl, it would have made some sense, but… anyway, I had no option but to follow the instructions.

I went to meet Anuradha's father Shri C P Sharmaji at Dehradun. He was working in a government department. So he, as the father of the girl, interviewed me for almost an hour. Post-marriage, he particularly expressed admiration for my self-confidence which he saw in me during the interview.

That's that! After matching our horoscopes, we tied the knot in 1986. I am thankful to God for granting me life partner who has been with me at every step of my life till now. I always had her love and company in all the joys and sorrows and ups and downs of life. I didn't even notice how fast this period of 37 years had passed.

This is how my parents' wishes were fulfilled. Now came a turning point in my life.

Now, my father, Anu, and I were living in the house I had built. Apologies for missing out on the fact that we had installed a gobar gas plant in our backyard. This is emblematic of my habit of never shying away from taking risks. I never hesitated. Whenever a new venture or idea crossed my mind, I'd formulate a plan and invest all my efforts to achieve it. I had even run a poultry farm for some time. These projects date back to the period before my marriage. In other words, they were parts of my résumé when I first met my father-in-law with the proposal to marry Anuradha!

My house built on the land bought by me;
The gobar gas plant also was located here.

Everything progressed smoothly, and time blessed me with a son, Abhishek, a year after marriage, followed by a daughter, Ankita, a year later. Both my children, by God's grace, are remarkable and understand their responsibilities. I take pride in both of them.

It is said that your happiness is determined not by your business but by your family; if you have peace and love at home, you would find love everywhere and everything else seems inconsequential. In this regard, I consider myself fortunate. We braved all the situations together.

At this point, I would like to share something, though reluctantly. My wife Anu discharged all the responsibilities of a homemaker and a life partner in the true sense. My wife was brought up in an urban environment, but she didn't hesitate to live with us in a village and left no stone unturned to take care of my father affectionately. Not only that, despite being used to making rotis on the gas stove, she would fire our earthen stove using a blowpipe and make rotis for us. Perhaps I could never express these feelings in front of her. How could I reveal my house affairs to the world? Hence, though reluctantly, I have mentioned this here. I swear to God, I feel blessed to have Anu in my life.

In the real sense, it was Anu who made our house a home and instilled in our children virtues in abundance. She was also always vigilant about the studies of our children. I remember there was one matter over which Anu would often get upset with me. Oh no! Don't be surprised. It wasn't a disagreement involving the two of us, but our son instead. We were discussing Abhishek's studies. She wanted us to shift to Dehradun to enroll him in a good school. When I placed this proposal before my father, he refused to leave his house and come to Dehradun. The matter was dropped there itself. However, when the same issue was raised by her the next day, I said I was willing to take a house in Dehradun and stay there with her and the children but I would go back to my father every night. She was very upset with me for that proposal. Before the matter went out of our control, we both discussed and agreed, rather I would say it was Anu's prudence, to get Abhishek admitted to any good boarding school at Dehradun. Thus, we got our son admitted to Colonel Brown Boarding School and we both stayed back with my father. We kept visiting our son in his hostel now and then.

All this started when Abhishek was just four and continued until he was around eight to nine years old. My father then said, "Jitender, you better build a house in Dehradun. I can't see you running around so much anymore." And so, I got into action, fulfilling my father's wish.

Anyway, this incident possibly relates to the year 2000. We will come back to this in the next chapter. For now, just be aware that the turning point of my life was just around the corner.

At this juncture, I also recollect another aspect. Our daughter, Ankita, like her brother, was admitted to St Mary Public School in Vikas Nagar. She completed her studies up to the sixth standard there. The memories of our family's growth, the joys, sorrows, and educational progress of our children are unforgettable. Every father goes through such experiences. Anyway, I've become a bit emotional. Let's continue..

Time is all-powerful! A critical test was just waiting for us. We all were badly unnerved. We can never forget that.

Our agarbatti powder business, flourishing with unwavering customer confidence, faced a sudden setback in 1988 when the government imposed a ban on cutting pine trees, the main source of our income. Moreover, our factory was also a means of employment for many. It felt like the ground was slipping away from under my feet. However, my father and Anu stood by me during this challenging time. “It’s the beginning of something still bigger, Jitender. God will not allow your perseverance to go to waste. Initially, I also wondered what you were doing; you could have pursued your studies and taken up some job. But today, I feel happy to see that you are the means for the livelihood of so many people. God will never take away your brightness. Have faith, there will definitely be some way out.”

And Anu, as if supporting me like a climber on a tree, said, “Don’t get disheartened. Have faith in God and your hard work. You are destined for something good. We are leading a comfortable life today thanks to your hard work and your willpower, and this will continue in the future too. I am always there with you in all your struggles."

I swear by God, all this filled me with tremendous energy, and I started planning for the future.

The company could not operate for a long time after that ban. After operating the factory for 1-2 years with the help of existing stock, it had to be closed. But my father was right in saying that something big was there on my way, and that's what happened. You may only stand up after falling... and I had already fallen. I was now going to stand up!

My focus now got redirected to some other activity. I will talk about that later.

Writing about oneself is undoubtedly challenging. I only realize that now. Every part of the past remains ingrained in us. Take a break, and let's meet in the next chapter with the continuing story.

❑

4

We Moved Ahead Again

As I look back at it now, it's remarkable how swiftly this prolonged period has passed. I never contemplated it before, just enduring whatever came my way without noticing time slipping by. However, now, as I've been penning down my life story for the past month, I've come to realize the significance of even the minutest details—regardless of whether they seemed meaningful at the time or not.

The next part of the journey of life will never be clear until its preceding part is explained properly. This explains why every action in our life is a prelude or foundation for the events to come.

When I began working on this book, I believed there would be only a few noteworthy events worth writing about. I envisioned jotting them down on a mere piece of paper and that would be my complete autobiography. Now, I understand that these major events were supported by innumerable smaller ones that escaped my attention. Thus, none of our actions is futile; there's always an outcome associated with them. And who I am today, and what I've achieved so far, is the result of these outcomes.

But enough of reflections; for now, let's return to where I left you in the previous chapter.

As I have already mentioned, the venture where I had put in all my efforts was going to come to an end. The situation also was different now. Earlier, I was alone... and could start or end anything at my will. I didn't have any major responsibility. But now, I was a father of two children. This kind of situation at this point in time was quite worrisome. But what was the option?

There was just one question now—what next?

After the government notification, all the companies started lowering their demands. What else could they have done? Earlier I used to be busy the whole day running here and there doing my work; sitting idly at home with everything suddenly coming to a standstill gave me a strange feeling.

I was at a loss to even think of anything. Suddenly I remembered something. My mother used to say something...

She would say, "Jitender, this world is a house built by God. There are umpteen doors in the same, and all of them are open and connected to each other. Hence, if you ever find things going wrong, don't get disheartened. Look around. You will find several paths that will take you forward. Just make sure you don't lose heart and keep trying."

These words of my mother did help me find a new path. I used to travel a lot in connection with my work, and I would keep meeting people during those travels. Even today, I am quick to make friends with people. As such, people even today say that anybody who meets me once does not forget me easily.

I just remembered one person who used to meet me often. He also used to travel most of the time. He was engaged in buying lands and selling plots. It's called the business of real estate—buying land and selling the same with some profit.

I had found my path. I extend gratitude to my close friend Dharm Singh Nakoti, who, though unknowingly and unintentionally, motivated me to take up this business. After making up my mind, I discussed this at home, understood the work involved and surveyed the market. I found the financials reasonable. So I decided to go ahead with the same. I invested whatever I had earned till that time. The machinery used for making *dhoop* powder was not of any use now. Hence, I sold the same for whatever price I got.

I was now fully involved in this work. Shortly, I rented a shop on the side of a road and converted that into my office. Thus, the foundation stone for my real estate business was laid in 1990. I also very soon realised one more thing. The work that looks easy and comfortable from the outside may not necessarily be so. One will only know the reality of that work when he performs the same himself. And that is not easy for everybody. The success of this entire business depends on the foundation of your diplomacy, patience and trust. The business would come to an end the day people lose trust in you.

Therefore, building and maintaining trust are crucial, requiring honesty in both words and actions. This was not too tough for me, as these qualities were already part of the morals that I had imbibed from my family.

The challenge in this business was its crowded nature, with several players already engaged. The question was, why would anybody come to me? Why would anybody trust me? Hence, I strategically opened my office at a location easily noticeable by people, confident that anyone who approached me would indeed do business. And that's precisely what happened!

And that's what happened! People gradually started coming to me. I also resolved to abide by the principle of working in a way that could win the trust of the people. 'Customer is God'—I always kept that in mind. I decided not to play with the trust of the people and never break their trust—even if that meant foregoing some comfort at home. This principle soon turned into my strength. Those who connected with me and executed deals would spread the word, and there came a time when my name resonated in the real estate business community. Isn't it a common saying that whatever you do, if you do the same diligently, God will not let you go empty-handed? I had the abundant blessings of God. He blessed us with plenty of happiness and prosperity. I also earned a lot—reputation as well as wealth.

It was my nature—I always believed in long-term relationships; if somebody got acquainted with me, I tried to ensure the relationship continued. Hence, I would not get upset even if a customer decided not to go ahead with the deal. I would treat all customers equally, as I knew even if a customer was not buying today, he would surely remember me, because of my dealings with him, whenever he planned to buy in the future. Didn't I tell you to have patience? This is what is called patience.

I would always pick up a customer on my scooter, offer him tea and snacks, show him plots, and then drop him back at the same spot. We would continue to remain in contact even if he didn't buy any plot.

Oh... that brings to my mind something about tea! My wife Anu makes excellent tea. So, whenever anyone visited our house in connection with the business, Anu would make tea for them and personally serve the same. Though we had servants at home, it was a cultural norm imbibed in most of our women to serve the guests, treating them akin to God. Anu would quite attentively honour, respect and serve the guests. It's the result of that devotion only that—today while writing this, I am just letting you know—those people still visit our house only to have tea made by Anu. Let's move ahead...

Now, let's talk about the scooter! I had a great fondness for scooters. During that time, things were different—scooters were not displayed in showrooms like they are today. Booking for new models would begin even before they hit the market. I would always book in advance and sell my old scooter to buy the new model.

My scooter and I.

The business was now well established. My brother Jagadish was always with me like *Lakshman*. A brother's company does provide a different level of courage.

Time was passing. The children had started to go to school, but I was so immersed in work and responsibilities that, even though I was at home, I could not spend much time there. I did my best, but being a father isn't easy.

My father was also having some health issues intermittently. However, whatever the situation, things were more or less manageable.

I didn't notice when the 20th century turned into the 21st. I bought and sold a number of plots. However, I had some vague feelings of dissatisfaction—though I had no idea why.

I had started in 1990; it was now the early 2000s. Meanwhile, as I said earlier, we shifted to Dehradun as per my father's wish. On Anu's suggestion, we got both our children admitted to the Asian School, Dehradun. Both the children made us proud and cleared their 10+2 examinations with good results. I was ecstatic and confident that they would complete their further studies successfully. Later, our son Abhishek completed his graduation and post-graduation from Garhwal University and went to London for his PhD. Our daughter Ankita also completed her graduation from St Bede's College, Shimla and and pursued an MBA in London.

The new year had arrived and people were exchanging greetings. But somehow, my mind appeared to be in a different mood. It appeared to be looking to reveal some shortcomings to me. I was not ready to listen. I was just procrastinating. But it's not possible to ignore your mind. And so, reluctantly, I listened to it.

It was telling me, "Jitender, you have done a lot of hard work and also attained success in the line of business you are currently in. But have you considered how people perceive you? A *Bhumafia*! Remember, you once held similar thoughts about the person who inspired you. Are you becoming what you once criticized?

"Would you continue to do the same thing; can't you take up something else? Isn't there anything better than this—something where you get some respect? Where people may remember you? You are now not lacking anything. You made good money, earned a lot, but..."

This shook me. There was chaos in my mind. I realised this was the cause of my dissatisfaction. My mind convinced me, and I silently made up my mind to do something new to create a fresh image for myself in the minds of people.

I had decided to shed my current image, to do something new. But what could I do for satisfaction?

Well, I finally found that. What that was—I will tell you after the break!

❑

5

Difficult But Attainable

God never lets us sit idle. There are always some activities unfolding in our lives. This ensures that we don't get stuck or sit idle at any particular point. God sometimes inspires us through successes and at other times awakens us through failures. Life is a continuous journey, a battlefield, and we must keep fighting.

I always feel that God presents challenges only to those whom he believes would make better use of them. Hence, I never get panicked by challenges; I face them head-on. I can say from my personal experience that whenever He presented any challenge before me and I persevered with my efforts, I was always rewarded with great success.

Otherwise, with the background I come from, I could have never dreamt of a life like the one I have today. All this is the result of my penchant for confronting the challenges in life. In other words, challenges are always meant to induce you to change tracks and improve them.

I don’t know exactly when I started the dairy business and how God kept blessing us always; despite so many ups and downs, many activities are flourishing today. Everything is changing around us. One change that was an opportunity for me in many respects was the carving out of the Uttaranchal region of Uttar Pradesh to create a new state of Uttarakhand. I now belonged to Uttarakhand, not Uttar Pradesh.

An idea to do something different had taken root in my mind. And amid such thoughts, I heard some voice from inside—'Barrister!'

My mother would always affectionately call me 'Barrister'. Probably, this very word was the means to pick out that different work for me. My mother had always pulled me out of similar situations. Today also, though she was not physically present, mentally she was always with me.

This word drew my attention to the education sector. What could be a better work than this—which could provide me happiness and also give me a chance to serve society? What's there in living for the self forever? If I had the capacity, why not do something for society? What could be a better charity than education?

Though I was just moderately educated, I realised its value. In our family, my elder brothers were highly educated.

I would consider my life to be meaningful if I could do something for the society in the education sector. With that thought, my mind was busy looking for some clues for my next step.

Finally, I had decided in which direction I had to move forward. But I was still unsure what exactly was to be done. Anyway, now that the direction was known, I was confident to find ways to proceed in that direction.

I discussed this with Anu at home. After all, she was my real adviser. Both Anu and I trusted each other absolutely. She knew that once Joshi Ji had resolved, he would not sit idle until the job was finished. I was aware of Anu's ability. She was managing the accounts for my real estate business. She was the one taking care of our two children and me. And she was also taking care of my father.

Now the question was—what to do next? And then suddenly, as before, something clicked in my mind—'Barrister'! Oh... great! I said, "How about opening a law college? What do you say?"

A thought came up in my mind. "*Ma*! I could not become a barrister, but now you just watch, how many barristers I am going to make!"

I got the support from my family. Now I started feeling that this was the job that would possibly fulfil whatever lack of satisfaction my mind had been experiencing and also give a new dimension to my image.

However, it was not an easy task—not like you thought about it and it was all done! I never start anything new with my eyes closed. I first study that work completely, interact with people in the relevant domain and then launch my venture after preparing a comprehensive and perfect plan.

It was true that this work was quite different from all the work I had handled before. When I discussed the plan with my friends in the real estate business, they discouraged me and wondered why I wanted to waste all my earnings on opening some school or college. They even cautioned it was not an easy venture, and after all, what was the need to go for it when everything was already going smoothly?

How could I tell them why it was required? I would have been a laughing stock then. It was work for my self-satisfaction. I just wanted to do something for the society now. More than my profits, this was meant for my peace.

I had to get rid of that tag that people attached to my name on my back.

And hence, I ensured such kinds of comments never made me weak. I decided to go ahead with the plan, no matter what happened.

I straight away went to schools and colleges. It gave me some idea as to how I should take my first step; and also that it was not going to be a cakewalk.

The first step I was required to take to open a college was to form a society. I submitted an application without any delay. Thinking of a name for the society, the first name that came to my mind and my lips was that of my mother. What could have been a better tribute from a son to his mother? With that, I would be able to perceive my mother's blessings and her presence close to me at every moment. I hence registered the society named after her—'Sushila Devi Centre for Professional Studies and Research'. Shri Rajiv Sharma, who had taken a lot of effort along with me to form this society, was assigned the responsibility for the role of Secretary of the society.

I had already taken the first step. If only my mother was there to watch all this happening!

Ok, folks, it was just a trailer. Something tough was awaiting Joshi Ji! Envisioning a college and getting it ready to operate—the journey between the two was not that short. Somebody had to come forward to discern the enormity of the idea.

There were many questions about the curriculum for the courses of the law college, able teachers, the structure of the college, permission from the government and approval from BCI (The Bar Council of India) that made me think. But I had already decided; there was no question of backing off. I proceeded to take the blessings of Kedar Baba. Kedar Baba is always with me.

I was putting in my best effort. I constantly interacted with people in the top law institutes and law universities in the country. I tried to understand everything necessary to establish a college as a top law college and university. I have told you this some 2-3 times... are you getting the point? It was not easy for Joshi Ji to go through all this. Ha ha ha!

And then one day, my efforts bore fruit! I was successful in having a meeting with Professor Govind Prasad Sharmaji of the Law Department at Hemvati Nandan Bahuguna University. My interaction with him provided a shape to the path of establishing the law college. He was an expert in his field. He had a thorough knowledge of all aspects right from the operation of the Law Department to the subjects of law. His experience came in very handy for me, as I was quite ignorant of this domain. I always remember him with gratitude.

My goal was to make the college a top-class institute. I had to make able barristers for the country.

I didn't want to leave any kind of flaw in the design of the college—right from its building to the level of teaching. I was doing whatever I could to ensure that.

To tell you the truth, there were occasions when I found my mind wavering and remembered the words of my friends. For some moments, I would feel I was content with my previous business and why should I take this risk. But on every such occasion, the name 'Barrister' given by my mother would resonate deep inside my mind and it would invigorate me to take on all the challenges coming in the way. Joshi would get spirited! I would think—after having committed to this mission, I should not fear the consequences, come what may. The more I encountered obstacles along the way, the stronger would be my steps.

In the same course, I came to know that a degree in law could be pursued as a three-year course after graduation or as a five-year course after 10+2. It was a great opportunity for me to open a law college with a five-year course, as at that time, this five-year law degree programme was not available in Hemvati Nandan Bahuguna University as well as in the entire Uttarakhand and neighbouring districts of other states. Thus, our law college got the credit of being the first college in Uttarakhand to provide a five-year law degree programme. For me, it was a golden opportunity to start the college with this new curriculum, as at that time, only a three-year LLB course was available in Hemvati Nandan Bahuguna University as well as in the entire Uttarakhand and neighbouring districts of other states. I wanted to make this curriculum available in my college; students of the neighbouring districts and states would not have to go around looking for this course anymore. It endeavoured to make available a good curriculum, good education and better facilities to all those students who saw their future in the domain of law. For this, some experts and I buckled down and duly gathered information relating to curriculum, rules and regulations and subjects as per the criteria set by the Bar Council of India.

I had to establish the best institution, and I was not going to back off from whatever effort required for the same.

I had started my journey by selling milk; these challenges were too small to unnerve me!

This time I was not alone; along with the members of the newly constituted Sushila Devi Centre of Professional Studies and Research, I set out in an organised way for the next stage. We prepared a list. It was the list of names of all the top law colleges in the country; we had to go to these colleges and collect information. We started the work without losing any time. We visited several colleges like Government Law College, Mumbai, National University of Judicial Sciences, Kolkata, West Bengal, Campus Law Centre, Delhi, National Law School of India University, Bangalore and Nalsar University of Law, Hyderabad. We observed them closely and tried to understand all the major as well as the minutest details relating to them. We even talked to the professors there and deeply studied all the relevant information.

These law colleges and universities had been the breeding grounds for eminent lawyers right from the best chief justices to the greatest spokespersons and politicians. Hence, I collected information with all the finer details. After all, I also had to produce worthy barristers for the country in the future.

When I returned after travelling for about 15 days, I started working without any delay on what I had understood and learnt.

Now it was time to decide the name of the college. I felt that Dehradun had been my *'karmbhoomi'*. It had helped me script a rags-to-riches story of my life. It gave me everything that a child born in a remote village of Uttarakhand cannot even imagine. I decided to name my college after Dehradun, and hence it was named 'Law College, Dehradun' (LCD).

Now another point came up for discussion that the college should have its own logo with a meaningful motto. In fact, there was a flurry of thoughts in my mind regarding this. There was serious brainstorming in my family and among my colleagues associated with this significant project. I must mention that I have inherited faith in God and belief in religion from my family. I had heard that in ancient times, 'law' was known as '*Dharma*'. I believe that everything is centred on religion. So, that was it. This idea was approved and the motto of the college was decided upon—*'Dharma Sarva Pratisthanam'*. I sincerely believe that whatever it meant, the feeling behind it was that wherever the students would go after studying here, they should be righteous in their conduct and that they should progress a lot and gain respect.

As it happens, there are some relationships in life whose love and support make the path of life easier. A home is created by relationships that are filled with love. A home is something that stays by your side through every sorrow and joy.

My wife Anu is very passionate about education. She gave me her complete support in my journey to build the law college. One day she said, "In our country, the number of girls who come forward as advocates to provide justice is far less than that of boys. Even today, the number of girls opting for law education is low. Why don't we work to awaken girls' interest in studying law and provide them with good facilities so that they can also receive a good education in law and become advocates and judges? For how long will they demand justice only for themselves? They should become so competent that they can help people get justice." I understood her concern for girls. At that time, I decided that female students would be paid special attention right from admission to study material or whatever other facilities that needed to be provided in the college.

Now there was one more point to consider, and that was what the medium of instruction should be.

However, I felt that most of the colleges that I had contacted offered the curriculum of law in English medium. I wanted to offer courses in Hindi medium along with English medium so that no one would find studying law difficult because of the language. But at that time, there was another opinion that the children's families also wanted their children to study in English medium only irrespective of the circumstances because the environment was in favour of English. English symbolised one's capability. But I thought of offering Hindi medium for students like me whose English is not so good or who want to study in their native language because I believe that language should never be an indicator of one's ability.

Thus, together, we made a decision that we would conduct courses in both the mediums. All the paperwork was completed with the help of the team. The college was upgraded on all the parameters that had to be presented to the government for permission to open a private college. There was no plan for a college at the time when Abhishek Tower was built. Today, it has proved to be of great use.

After inspection, permission to open the college on the third floor of Abhishek Tower was granted. If the permission had not been granted, then another building would have had to be built, and only then would the permission be granted. However, it was a relief that the investigation team found Abhishek Tower suitable for the college and granted the permission. Otherwise, a huge expense would have to be incurred.

I remember an incident related to Abhishek Tower. When Abhishek Tower was being built, my father had come to visit Dehradun. One day, I told my younger brother Jagdish to show our father whatever we had built there. Jagdish took my father on a tour of the properties that we had acquired in the Gypsy that we had bought.

By the grace of God, it took three to four days for my father to tour all the properties we had built. Jagdish told me that while exploring, my father repeatedly asked, "Has Jitender bought all of this?"

I am not writing all this here to show off. This is simply a son writing about his feelings for his father upon seeing the pride and joy in his eyes.

Similarly, what my father once said is what every son dreams of in life. When Abhishek Tower was ready, my father cut the ribbon during the inauguration ceremony of the tower. After that, he sat and relaxed. People standing nearby were talking among themselves. The invitees asked who the old man cutting the ribbon was. Then someone replied that he was Jitender Joshi Ji's father. They all looked at him with great respect. My father was filled with pride. I am not making this up. This was what my father told my younger brother: "Today, I felt very happy. Till now everyone knew him by my name, but today, everyone knows me by his name. Jitender is very hardworking. Both of you should keep working diligently in this way, cooperate with each other, and stay together. God is always with you."

This feels like my biggest earning. Whatever we do, if we cannot make our father proud of us, then we cannot call ourselves successful.

These are memorable moments for me. I could not get enough time with my father. His health was not quite good. On 30 November 2000, he left for his heavenly abode. My father had worked very hard all his life. He nurtured and educated all of us siblings while working in a small job. Everything was because of him. Today my father is not with us. But I am satisfied that before his demise, I could repay a part of my debt to him by sending him on the *Char Dham Yatra* as per the beliefs of the Hindu religion where one is required to complete the *Char Dham Yatra* for a fruitful life on earth.

When my father would sit on the terrace and see a helicopter flying, he would say to me, "I have never sat in a helicopter." I had engraved this wish of his in my mind. I am happy that I took him in a helicopter to see the representation of the bravery of my country during the Republic Day parade at Rajpath in Delhi on 26 January. I cannot express in words the happiness that appeared on his face after boarding the helicopter. When I remember that happy face, I always feel zestful.

Sometimes, when our views did not match, he would also admonish me. He wanted me to find a job and become financially secure. But my goal was entirely different. However, I fulfilled my goal when he was around and made him proud. I consider this my biggest success.

For a long time, I didn't like to be at home. Whenever I entered the house, I saw my father sitting on the porch. He would always say, "Where do you roam all day long? Sometimes, you should try staying at home, too." All these have become memories now. But are we left with any option other than accepting the truth and moving forward? This is life. However, memories keep taking you back to the past.

Anyway, that is how it was meant to happen. Well, after treasuring my father's memories, let us turn our attention towards the law college again. We decided to have uniforms for the students, although, at that time, most of the colleges did not have uniforms. The decision was prompted by my wife Anu's opinion. She was of the view that uniforms were necessary because it would prevent discrimination between rich and poor as many times children feel inferior because of their clothes. Therefore, if everyone wore similar kinds of clothes, then there would be no discrimination. I understood what she meant.

Preparations for starting the law college were in the final stage. Now it was the time to seek permission from the Uttarakhand Government to start the college. It was not an easy task. But as someone has said—when the purpose is noble and the intention is pure, then God himself paves the way for you. The same happened in my case, too. There were difficulties at every step. But as we know—all's well that ends well. And I had the letter with the permission to start law college in my hands. The happiness of me and my colleagues knew no bounds.

In this way, my dream college was ready in its form. Now I had to approach the Bar Council of India for approval of affiliation. I had the file prepared as per the guidelines and send the file to the office of the Delhi, Bar Council of India. I can never forget 30 June 2002, when the team from the Bar Council of India conducted the first inspection of Law College, Dehradun. We were all edgy but confident. Anu repeatedly assured me that I had done all the work with complete honesty and that no power could now stop our college from opening. And that is what happened—I received permission and another dream of mine was fulfilled.

All of my tasks were completed. Now it was time to inaugurate the college and start the classes. The then governor of Uttarakhand, Shri Surjit Singh Barnala, who had an unassuming personality, gave his approval for the inauguration of the college. Shri Ramesh Pokhriyal 'Nishank', who was the cabinet minister in the Uttarakhand Government and who had extended his full support in making this college a reality, also gave his consent. The formal inauguration was decided to take place in the month of October.

Mr. Surjit Singh Barnala, the dedicated Governor of Uttarakhand, inaugurates the Law College

I still remember the day of 1 August 2002, when the session was to start. I entrusted the responsibility of conducting the inaugural class of Law College, Dehradun to my closest colleague, Dr Rajesh Bahuguna.

I had never imagined that the small sapling of Law College, Dehradun, would grow into a banyan tree of 'Uttaranchal University' as I write this book.

I felt immense satisfaction. Moreover, I was thrilled when all the seats in both three-year and five-year courses were filled during the very first year of my dream college. The dedication of the teachers, staff, and students quickly elevated my law college to one of the best institutions in Uttarakhand. This success boosted my morale, affirming my belief in my ability to work in this field. So, I did not stop.

I expanded the college beyond law, introducing many non-technical and technical courses. As the number of students grew, Abhishek Tower could no longer accommodate them. Without delay, the college was shifted to Prem Nagar, Dehradun.

Performing Bhoomi Pujan for the reestablishment of the Law College at Premnagar.

You might be wondering about my real estate business. I did not close it; it continued to thrive. The substantial income from the real estate business was crucial for undertaking the massive project of the college. However, as my interest shifted more towards the college, I handed over the responsibility of running the real estate business to my younger brother, Jagdish. My days were consumed by college-related work, and I found peace and true success in that.

In this way, the law college was started and within a short time, colleges offering many other courses were also opened. However, small and big challenges kept cropping up every now and then. A few pages will not suffice to describe them. I have not written much here. What can one say about this? The bigger the dream, the more difficulties there will be... It is normal.

My friends who counted the problems in the project to me were now full of praise after everything went well. From this experience, I understood one thing, which you should also understand, that if the objective is righteous, one should go ahead because the experience of every undertaking is different. If a project ever fails, it does not necessarily mean it can never be accomplished. Time brings with it its own capabilities and opportunities.

I was very happy. It took time and struggle, but it was successful.

Well, there are still many things to tell further in the story, and I will not let you go without telling you about them. I don't like to leave both the job and the discussion incomplete.

I do not stop without putting a full stop. Ha...ha...ha.

Receiving Amar Ujala Achievers Award-2018 by Her Excellency the Governor, Honorable Smt. Baby Rani Maurya

Receiving 'Uttarakhand Shi Samman' from Chief Minister Shri Pushkar Singh Dhami

Receiving 'Jagran Excellence Award 2018' from Honorable Chief Minister Uttarakhand, Shri Trivendra Singh Rawatji'

Receiving ASSOCHAM National Education Excellence Award from Honorable Cabinet Minister Dr. Karna Singh

Chief Minister Vijay Bahuguna giving away awards to the winners in the National Uttarakhand Education Award program organized by CMAI at Survey Auditorium, February 11, 2013

Receiving 'Most Aware Campus of Uttarakhand' Award from Honorable Higher Education Minister, Uttarakhand, Shri Dhan Singh Rawatji

Receiving Brand Icon Award from Respected Acharya Balkrishna Ji

Receiving 'Uttarakhand Uday Award – 2017' from Honorable Chief Minister Uttarakhand, Shri Trivendra Singh Rawatji

Receiving 'Visionaries of Uttarakhand Award' by Honorable Chief Minister Shri Vijay Bahuguna

Receiving 'Uttarakhand Ratna Award' from Former Governor Punjab, Honorable Justice O.P. Jindalji.

Receiving 'Most Promising Engineering and Most Promising Management Institute Award' from Honorable Minister of State for Human Resources and Development Shri Upendra Khushwahaji

Receiving the State Level Education Excellence Award in the dignified presence of Honorable Cabinet Ministers Shri Prakash Pantji and Shri Subodh Uniyalji along with Nyaya Murthy Shri Rajesh Tandonji

6

Our Orchards and Social Reforms

So, you are back! Very good! You are not getting bored, are you? I can't believe that I have already written so many chapters. While writing, I keep forgetting that I am 62 years old. I feel I am the same age or at that stage of life that I am writing about. Every scene unfolds one by one as if a movie is playing.

So, let's move ahead. Where was I? Yes... by now we have completed the journey of the college opening. Things were going great there. I would often visit classrooms, talk to students, and inspire them with my experiences in whichever way I could.

Now I will talk further about what I wrote in the previous chapters when I said that I was very fond of gardening. I also mentioned that I had purchased a mango orchard of 200 *bighas*. It was my hobby, and I was also getting income from the selling of mangoes. It is still continuing. I often go there whenever I feel like it. I sit there for a while and have discussions with my associates who live there. All in all, it means that I love gardening.

This very hobby of mine was forming a new goal for me in my life journey.

Now let me think where I should start narrating this part.

It so happened that I went to Shimla on a trip with my friends from Dehradun. Although nature has blessed Dehradun in its full beauty, Shimla, being a hill station, offers a unique charm. Witnessing the scenery, it seemed that nature has bestowed upon us numerous priceless gifts, on which no value or price can be put. How splendid this world is! Actually, it is far beyond imagination. This beauty of nature and its fragrance invade our senses and gratify the inner soul. When Mother Earth gets drenched with drops of rain, the heart is filled with love and starts counting the golden memories of life. There are so many memories, cherished in some corner of the heart, that come alive with the rains.

Nature gives us so much without expecting anything from us. Appreciating these qualities of nature, I went on a trip with my friends from Dehradun to relish the beautiful views of nature and the golden snowy valleys of Shimla in Himachal Pradesh. It was around the month of August 2004. It was evening by the time we reached Shimla. We checked the arrangements for accommodation and went to the Himachal Guest House in Fagu to spend the night. A warm bonfire glowed in the courtyard, offering respite to those seeking refuge from the cold weather. We had to leave in the morning to visit the temple and the places of natural scenery. Drifting into slumber, the vivid memory of that serene scene accompanied our dreams.

The next day, early in the morning, I stood near the window of my room, from where the view outside the guest house could be seen—the rising sun of Shimla, cold weather, and people strolling. I stood there looking at them for a while.

I wanted to start the day by visiting the *Hanuman* temple located there. After taking a bath, we left for *Hanumanji's darshan*. After the *darshan* at the temple, we moved ahead, full of new energy.

We wanted to visit the various beautiful valleys of Shimla. We were engrossed in the views of the beautiful valleys from Sanjauli to Dhalli. The cool breeze caressing the face buoyed the mind. The high hills, the roads passing through those hills, the rays of the sun peeking through those roads, and the soft sunlight seemed to add beauty to nature. Really, these beautiful and captivating natural views of the valleys from Sanjauli to Dhalli and Dhalli to Fagu were a sight to behold. As we were strolling, we reached a tea shop. Tea in the early morning and that too in Shimla is a different kind of pleasure. A gentleman wearing a Himachali cap was brewing tea at the shop. As we sipped tea, we chatted and spoke, admiring Shimla. After having our tea and breakfast, we set out again for a stroll.

The more closely we get to know nature, the more we feel happy. One felt at peace in these valleys. While walking, one particular sight amidst the views of these beautiful valleys caught my attention. I saw orchards laden with apples. As far as my eyes could see, there were beautiful apple orchards. Every apple tree was laden with beautiful red apples. I stood there admiring the beauty of the orchards. That view captivated me so much that I greedily stored it in my eyes and mind. As I walked through the apple orchards, I gradually became curious to know how this work was carried out. Since I have also planted mango orchards, I could guess it was certainly not an easy task. Besides, it seemed to me that this required more care and attention than mango cultivation. My mind had started working. I wanted to meet the owners and people working on those plantations. I wanted to understand this job.

They were doing a great job. I saw some people working in an orchard nearby. I approached them, introduced myself, and conversed with them. I felt a different kind of joy after talking to them. Their love, warmth, and hard work in the apple orchards encouraged me a lot. The apple orchards seemed to have settled in my mind.

I was living the journey. This journey was bringing to the fore many thoughts and questions lying dormant within me. Seriously, I wanted to lose myself in these valleys. Who says mountains are quiet and lonesome? They are full of love. You can find such solitude and peace here. These valleys and gardens filled every corner of my mind with tenderness. It was as if a new awareness was occupying the space. It was almost evening. The cool breezes created an altogether different atmosphere. The colourful rays of the sun peeping through the mountains gave a gentle glow, making one aware of the end of the day. Flocks of birds were returning home after travelling miles afar. We also decided to return to our guest house in Fagu. But my mind and thoughts were occupied by apple orchards. I wanted to do something about it. We returned to the guest house. After resting for some time, we decided to sit near the fire burning outside. A few people were sitting near the fire and chatting. I also went and sat there. There was a radio nearby that played old songs which gave a feeling of warmth in the cold of the evening. Many thoughts rushed through my mind like a boat stuck in the middle of a river, which wanted to reach the shore. I was thinking about those orchards. The night had deepened. The songs on the radio had stopped playing. The flames of the fire had died down. We went to our respective rooms. I fell asleep thinking of those sights filled with golden memories.

The next day, we planned to go in the other direction for a stroll. We decided to go to Jubbal Valley. We started the day with breakfast and tea and then left for Jubbal Valley. There, the beauty of nature shone with a different lustre. If you have never been there, my words may seem filmy to you. But everyone experiences this after coming here.

The cold winds prickled the arms and became a memory. The eyes beheld the beautiful scene serenely. Those calm, beautiful green hills that touched the sky seemed to be holding a quiet conversation. Come to think of it, such beauty had been my companion through every moment from childhood till adulthood. The valleys of Dehradun were no less stunning. But actually, the beauty of this place is etched in my memory to date. I saw large apple orchards here as well. Every tree was laden with clusters of beautiful red apples. Every plant there was pulling me towards itself. I made up my mind that I had to do something. It is said that when you have a dream and want to achieve it, then first of all, you should lay its foundation and then give up your sleep, fear and lethargy and work with full dedication to achieve it. Then you will definitely be successful. And if you still don't get the desired success, you won't return empty-handed.

Having read this far, you must have understood one thing about me I've diligently toiled for every dream conceived in my life and, gratifyingly, turned them into tangible achievements.

Today, a new dream of mine took birth in these valleys—to plant an apple orchard in the valleys of Shimla. When I shared this dream with my friends who had come with me, they said that since we were there for a pleasure trip, we should enjoy it to the fullest and not think of other things. They said it did not make sense to buy an apple orchard away from Dehradun, and then again, it required different skills. It was an apple orchard and not a mango one! There was a lot of difference between the two. Everyone kept saying such things.

But by now, you also know that once Joshi Ji decides something, it definitely takes some form. I have lived my childhood through many ups and downs, crossing rocky paths. At that time, too, I never missed any opportunity. And now the success in starting a college also boosted my self-confidence. I didn't know anything even then... but it happened... just like that... that's it! I thought—why not give it a try? Life had shown me a new goal that day. I thought to myself: who knows something good might come out of it. I sat down with the owner of an apple orchard in an area where I had gone for a stroll. He ordered tea. While drinking tea, I told him about my desire. I said, "Sir, I found the apple orchards here very delightful. I also own a small mango orchard in Dehradun. I feel I should also try my hand at an apple orchard here." He laughed and said, "Joshi Ji, it is definitely possible. But for that, you will have to marry an orchard owner's daughter here. If you give your consent, we will take this forward."

Everyone there started laughing. He had said this jokingly, but he wanted to explain the law of Himachal Pradesh through this. Then he told me that people from other states cannot buy land there. One cannot become a resident of the state just like that. Therefore, if someone gets married into a family here, then he naturally gets the right to buy land and plant a field.

When he told me all this, my entire plan came crumbling down. Alas! What could I do now...! I felt as if the apple orchard would only remain a dream for me. The law of Himachal Pradesh had proven to be a huge obstacle in my dream. When I called my lawyers based in Dehradun and asked for their advice, they also validated this law of Himachal Pradesh and told me that since I was a resident of Uttarakhand, I could neither buy an orchard nor an agricultural land under the law of Himachal Pradesh.

Those beautiful moments and gorgeous apple orchards had become very precious to me. I did not want to let go of them. I felt miserable. Perhaps my friends accompanying me could also see this insipid mood of mine. After touring the beautiful valleys and apple orchards of Himachal with my friends for about 15 days, I returned to Dehradun in the month of August. The dream of apple orchards constantly made its presence felt in my eyes and heart.

When I was going through struggles in my life, my father gave me some great advice: To attain a new position, always keep the desire to achieve your goal in front of your eyes and heart. Work with such intensity that you won't even need your father's support. Forge a new identity for yourself, independently! Then one day when I was sitting immersed in thoughts, a song from *Mother India* played on TV.

The lyrics were:

"Duniya mein hum aye hain to jeena hi padega
Jeevan hai agar jahar toh peena hi padega."

(Since we have taken birth into this world, we have to go on living. Even if life is poison, we have no choice but to drink it.)

When I heard the song, a voice from my heart said, "Joshi...

Than le insan toh kya kaam hai mushkil
Duniya mein hum aye hain to jeena hi padega."

(No task is difficult when a person is determined,

Since we have taken birth into this world, we have to go on living.)

My father's teachings and that song helped me stand up again. I thought of a way. I remembered that the border of Uttarakhand and Himachal lay along the lines of those apple orchards and apples are cultivated there, too. Therefore, one could own an orchard in Uttarakhand if not in Himachal. There was no such rule here. I had decided to cultivate apples with full confidence and I wanted to fulfil it with the same confidence. I would meet a number of people every day and seek information about cultivating apples, the weather needed, and maintenance. It is said that when you undertake any task with great devotion, God also fully supports you in your journey.

Without further delay, I went to visit the village on the border of Himachal Pradesh and Uttarakhand, where apple is cultivated.

Now you might be wondering why should you have apple orchards only there. Why can't you cultivate apples in Dehradun itself?

Now, you must understand... Apples require a cold climate and environment, which Dehradun does not have. The colder the climate, the better the quality of the apples... That's why apple orchards can be planted only where there is snow, and they are of really good quality. Therefore, to get the full benefit of snow, higher locations are chosen for apples. So, I had to look for all these aspects of the cultivation of apples. Hence, I was looking for apple orchards in Uttarakhand that were at the same height as Shimla.

In the journey of life, we meet some people with whom we are not related by blood, but that relationship is a precious gift from God, which is a wonder in itself. In the same way, one day, I met my family friend Pritam Singh Rawatji. He introduced me to Shri Malchand, who was the elected MLA of Purola Assembly, Uttarkashi district. I told him about my dream of owning an apple orchard and my efforts to fulfil it. He appreciated me for that and introduced me to one of his friends, Shishupal Singh Rawat. After serving in the Indo-Tibetan Border Police services, Shishupal Singh Rawat had retired and started farming with his wife Balbiri Rawat, a hardworking woman of simple nature, in his native Kunara village, Mori tehsil, Uttarkashi district. His father Sunder Singhji was also fond of apple orchards, and he had planted an apple orchard in the same village of Kunara. Shishupal Singh also kept himself busy in the maintenance of that orchard. Shishupal Singh, a man of simple nature and honest personality, also had good knowledge of apple gardening. Sometimes, many things in life seem like miracles. These miracles are brought about by God himself. The meeting with Shishupal Singhji was no less than a miracle for me towards realising my dream of having an orchard. The meeting with Rawatji and his wife awakened a new energy in me.

Now I had to struggle for a new task. It was a struggle which could bring about a change in Uttarakhand. In 2005, I, along with Shishupal Singh Rawatji, bought an orchard of 400 *nali* between village Kunara and Rudrala (Kharasa) in Mori development block of Uttarkashi district from Shri Mirchuramji, who was the resident of Himachal Pradesh. Along with this, I also made another decision. I thought that when the world was moving towards organic fertilisers, then why not use completely organic fertilisers in apple orchards? When it comes to organic farming, I remember one thing—to make organic fertiliser a reality, I reared two hundred and fifty goats. We prepared compost from the waste of those goats and started using it as an organic fertiliser. So, we raised the plants in our orchard through organic fertilisers. We prepared compost using cow dung and legitimately developed apple orchards. We cultivated apples of the Royal variety in the orchards. I often used to go to the Uttarkashi Mori development block from Dehradun. When I saw labourers working in the orchard, I would also help them. I always met them cordially and spent time with them in the orchard.

For me, this was my golden dream, which I saw flourishing in front of my eyes, and for which I was making every possible effort. At last, the day came when the first lot of apples emerged from the orchard. I felt immense happiness upon seeing the harvest. After all, this was what I had dreamt of in the valleys of Fagu and Dhalli of Himachal. The dream, the desire that I had nurtured in my eyes and heart at that time, had finally become a reality.

I was grateful to God for this. I also thanked the labourers who had nurtured that orchard with so much affection. I gifted those apples to my friends in Dehradun. They were also astonished at my success. Everyone appreciated and congratulated me. That day, I realised that if you want to win, you have to keep your dream alive in your heart and struggle for it until it becomes a reality. However, my struggle was far from over. I still had more dreams, and I wanted to soar higher.

Me and My Orchards

Shishupal Singh Rawat's wife Balbiri Devi started taking care of this 400 *nali* orchard located in the development block of Mori with the help of Panch Dera Nepalis. I took further steps. In 2007, together with Rawatji, I made a deal for another 25 *bighas* of land in his village of Rudrala, where I had plans to plant apple and pear trees. The responsibility of taking care of this orchard also fell on him. This land spread over 25 *bighas* was known as 'Bandi'. When I took a step towards my next milestone, I knew that in the future, I would have to face many new challenges. The next challenge for me was the new variety of high-quality apples from Himachal Pradesh. Scientists at the Apple Research Centre, Himachal Pradesh prepared high-quality apple varieties on the lines of Germany and Europe, whose enhanced plants were bearing fruits before usual time. Those fruits were being delivered to the market in July-August. There was a lot of demand for them in the market, and they also started fetching good prices. On the other hand, the variety of apples grown in the orchards of Uttarkashi was not of advanced quality and the harvest was also late, due to which it did not fetch a fair price in the market.

The real challenges for me were going to come now. But amid these challenges, I never let my dreams fade from my sight. There was going to be a new turn in apple cultivation. Now the challenge for me was to find out the effect the soil of Uttarkashi would have on the advanced varieties of plants that the Apple Research Centre, Himachal Pradesh had prepared for the gardeners of their state. I had a lot of questions. I wanted to bring these improved varieties to the land of Uttarkashi. It was a challenging task. But I moved ahead with a positive attitude and landed at the Govind Ballabh Pant University of Agriculture and Technology located in Pant Nagar of Udham Singh Nagar district of Uttarakhand, which was established by the country's first Prime Minister Pt Jawaharlal Nehru in 1960, which is today considered a Green Revolution industry.

There is a Plant Nutrition Laboratory here, which used to work for sugarcane research. I decided to take the help of the scientists here to take an advanced course on horticulture. I went to Pant Nagar, met the scientists, and gave them the soil from my orchard for testing. Additionally, during this period, I also visited countries in Europe and tried to understand the technology of developing improved varieties of apples. I also took appropriate advice from the scientists there and decided to bring several samples and develop them in the soil of Uttarkashi. The scientists in the university, with their complete technical knowledge, helped in the development of new and improved varieties of apples through their research.

On the advice of scientists, I decided to replant my apple orchard located in the Mori development block of Uttarkashi in 2009 and planted the apple trees of advanced species developed through research. Their names are Super Chief, Gale Gala, Red Chief, Jeromine and Scarlet-2. These apple varieties were made capable of blooming in the land of Uttarkashi through research on improved varieties from Germany and Europe. In this process, I received full support from the scientists of the country's first Dr Yashwant Singh Parmar Horticulture and Forestry University located in Solan, Himachal Pradesh. Today, I realise that the paths in life are never straight. A new challenge lurks at every turn. But if you look forward to the destination with enthusiasm, then you will not even know when you will have left these challenges behind and when a new path opens up ahead, provided that you have worked diligently with a positive attitude.

Today in our orchard, with the help of scientists at the university, improved varieties of pear along with apple have been developed. They have been planted along with apples in Bandi village. As a result of hard work, today along with apple trees, about 1,000 pear trees are also flourishing in this garden. They include improved varieties of pear such as Concord, Green Enjay, Starkrimson, and Bartlett. This orchard is also being taken care of by *Two Dera* Nepalis under the guidance of Mrs Balbiri Deviji. Today, as I am writing my own dreams, I finally understand that tireless efforts have been made to make every dream come true. Perhaps that is why these fruits not only taste sweet but very sweet.

Every year, apple trees are trimmed in the months of January and February. To heal the wounds that occur in plants as a result of trimming, a paste of copper, linseed oil, and vermilion is applied to them. To protect the sprouting buds from ants, lime is applied on the trunks of the trees, and fungicides and multivitamins are also sprayed from time to time. It is true that these trees also need to be nurtured like children. It is only then that such orchards grow. So much has to be done for them! They need to be taken care of in every possible way. Only then do apples taste so good.

During these 5-6 years of apple gardening, Shishupal Singh Rawatji and I developed a very close bond. This journey continued. In 2010, I purchased another piece of land measuring 40 *bighas* in the village of Haltadi from the villagers there. In the year 2011-12, various varieties of apple were developed and about 4,000 saplings were planted, which were now included in the samples. This orchard is being taken care of by Shishupal Singh along with Santosh Rangad, who is a resident of that area, and *Two Dera* Nepalis. A guest house has also been built from cedar wood in this orchard. Whenever I or my family members go to the orchard in Mori development block, we stay there.

Our guest House in our Gardens

A dream that I saw on the soil of Himachal Pradesh in the year 2004-05 has become a reality today. My dream of owning an orchard has made me the biggest horticulturist not only in Uttarakhand but also in Himachal Pradesh. Hardly anyone here has around 25,000 apple trees of such range and advanced varieties. The result of this is that apple orchards have become an industry today. The biggest outcome that makes me happy is that this development in the mountains of Uttarkashi has also succeeded in stopping the migration of people. I don't think there can be any greater happiness in life than being able to support someone and contribute to their happiness. For me, the real gift that I have received in return for my work is the happiness on the faces of those people, which they got in the form of employment, which could stop their migration. I also distributed grafts of my improved varieties of apples and pears to the villagers for free, with the help of which small farmers started rearing the improved varieties of apples and pears, thereby raising their standard of living. It also stopped them from migrating.

To be honest, dreaming about an orchard and its journey up to this point is like a precious gift from God to me. The orchard purchased in Swinchan village has more than 2,500 trees of advanced species. This garden has been developed as a sample model. Apple growers from far and wide visit this orchard and learn about modern technology.

During one's journey of life, there come such turns on the way that sometimes give you a new identity forever. The same thing happened to me during my trip to Himachal, which gave me a new identity.

So, this was the story of my apple gardening. By the end of this story, you may have felt quite bored. But I wrote it with the thought that it would be of great use to those who might be interested in it.

Please understand one thing... No matter how big a goal is, never blindly follow anyone's advice. It is not necessary that if it is difficult for them, it should also be difficult for you. Try it and then make a decision.

So, now you know about my passion for horticulture as well. It is time to move on to the next part...

❑

7

From School to University

There is no end to our desires, a sentiment often echoed in sermons and *satsangs*. We keep hearing that desires never die. We must exercise control over them. This last line is significant. We do not pay attention to it. There has never been any mention of ending desires. If that were so, this world wouldn't progress. I firmly believe that desires directed towards public and social welfare are always worthy. Hence, we should strive to fulfill our desires, especially those with noble intentions. Such aspirations, aimed at contributing to the greater good, should be enduring.

I am not as wise as what I expressed above. I apologise if I said something inappropriate. When I sat down to write this chapter, this thought went through my mind because there was no end to my desires either.

Initially, I wanted to create a new image by giving something to society, and it was with this purpose that I opened the law college. Then as my desires as well as the demands of time grew, I opened engineering and management colleges one by one.

And now with the excellent performance of the students studying in our institutes, my desire to do more in the field of education grew further. I probably wouldn't stop here either.

The story was going to continue. Now, not just a college but a university was going to be opened.

To be honest, I never thought that so many colleges would be opened and that the idea of a university would be conceived. But a great man has said that the process of progress starts when you start with whatever comes to your mind and feels good. Do not think about how difficult it is. Gradually, you will achieve it. If you get scared just by thinking how difficult it is, then you will not be able to start in the first place. If fear of difficulty hinders you from starting, someone else might realize the dreams you aspired to, right before your eyes. At that time, you will not be able to do anything else except regret that it would have been better if you had done it!

I felt good thinking that I had done well by taking a step forward. Otherwise, after continuously listening to what people said, I was going to step back. Well, in the end, I did gather courage. I think this courage was the result of my mother's constant encouragement. She would say, "Jeetu, you should do everything with full dedication, and you should not panic under any circumstances."

Now, let me tell you how the idea of the university took birth.

As I have already mentioned, a law college was opened in the year 2002 after a lot of struggles. During the very first year, all the seats for three-year and five-year courses were filled. Due to the hard work of excellent teachers and officials, the very first batch made a mark at the university level, with nine out of the top ten students hailing from our college. This success boosted the morale of all of us, and our student also won the gold medal of the university. Our happiness knew no bounds. My team and I were filled with tremendous enthusiasm.

When we started facing space constraints in Abhishek Tower with the rise in the number of students, we constructed a building in Arcadia Grant, Prem Nagar. Here, I will tell you about the idea of constructing a building for the law college...

I told my architect Mr Alok Pandey that the building should be constructed in such a way that its very sight would be pleasing to the mind and that it should be filled with such energy that every being would be eager to learn something there. I also said to him that it should be built in such a way that more similar buildings could be built in the future. I don't know why I said that. Perhaps the mind unwittingly perceives the future. Little did I know then that this vision would manifest into 16 academic buildings, 14 hostels, and a guest house across 55-56 acres.

There is one more thing, which I think I should tell you. The thing is that I wasted almost 100 litres of paint just to choose the colour for the building! After mixing many colours, the final colour that appeared on the building brought joy to my face. I wrote down the combination in one of my diaries, which is the colour of the building as it stands today.

I am writing all this here because all of us need to plan and then think a lot and work hard to complete it so that the results give happiness. As a matter of fact, proper planning is the key to success. It is possible that we may have to see many failures during the process. But success is the result of not giving up.

So, let's go back to the university.

It so happened that after the results of the first batch of students were declared, I, looking at the progress in the technical and management fields in society and their future, decided that along with providing law education, technology, and management should also be taught. In 2006, 'Uttaranchal Institute of Management' and 'Uttaranchal Institute of Technology' were affiliated with Uttarakhand Technical University. We further strengthened our team by recruiting good teachers.

The hard work started paying off, and the number of students continuously increased in our three institutes. I was content and thanked God daily for his blessings.

Let me share something with you. No, it wasn't anything extraordinary, but it's often said that when something good and substantial is about to happen, obstacles inevitably arise.

Due to the separate associations between the three colleges and the two universities and the distance between them, my team, who used to get the work done at the universities, had to work twice as hard. Every task of the college related to administration and education had to be done at the university. Sometimes it was related to admissions, examinations, mark sheets, and degrees, and at other times it was about bringing paper-copy at the time of examination and returning it within the stipulated time. Colleges had to do everything within the timeframe allotted by the universities. It was becoming difficult to travel like this. Nevertheless, everything was going well with my mother's blessings and God's grace. However, in 2012, a thought flashed through my mind—why not open my own university?

Now, this thought was not a big deal for me because till now I had accomplished whatever I had planned. I kept thinking that in order to run these colleges efficiently, I or my team members should not have to commute or travel constantly. This idea became the foundation of the university in my mind, and I joined hands with the entire team to make it a reality. Now, you know my habit. I started working hard to collect every small and big detail about building the university and I continued to collect all the information for six months.

Now the question arose—what should be the name of the university? I thought that the names of my two colleges were 'Uttaranchal Institute of Management' and 'Uttaranchal Institute of Technology'. I liked Uttaranchal because I was born and brought up in Uttaranchal. Everyone loves their birthplace. Before this area was carved out as a separate state from Uttar Pradesh, it was called Uttaranchal. Thus, I could not separate myself from Uttaranchal. It seemed as if I was losing a trace of my childhood. That is probably why I named my colleges after Uttaranchal. Even now I inadvertently say 'Uttaranchal' while talking.

I thought about it and took the final decision that the university would be named 'Uttaranchal University'. This is how the name of the university was born.

After the name was decided, I learnt about the entire process of the establishment of the university from many experts and had the necessary documents prepared. Then after completing all the formalities from our side, we sent them to the Ministry for application.

Whenever the Ministry asked us to improve or prepare any document, I completed the task without wasting any time. I had to go to many places to meet and talk to people. I explained my problems, spoke about the achievements of my colleges, and explained my objective.

I remember one incident. When I presented the proposal for the university to the government, Chief Minister Shri Vijay Bahuguna Ji asked me the final question, "Joshi Ji, what benefit will the state get from your university?"

I said, "We will reserve 40 percent of seats in the university for the students from our state. There will be up to 26 percent relaxation in their fees." The chief minister was happy to learn this.

I'm pleased to inform you that a few years after the university's opening, we started providing an additional 5 percent to girls. We also extended a 5 percent benefit to those belonging to families from the armed forces.

Finally, after some duration, the Uttaranchal University Act 2012 was passed and it was declared a university in 2013. This university has been successfully discharging its responsibilities. 'Uttaranchal University' is committed to providing better education to the children of the country and runs courses of all the faculties. It became the first university in Uttarakhand to be awarded NAAC A+ grade. Now, let us learn a little about my 12 colleges and their success stories.

Oh yes! There is one more thing. In the meantime, I opened a school in my father's name. While discussing the university, I forgot to mention it. Let me tell you about it, and then we will move ahead.

Ever since I grew up and became mature enough, I cannot bear to see anyone suffering. During my struggling days, if I saw someone approaching me on the street or anywhere else to ask for something, I would try to avoid them. Because they would ask for something that I would not be able to give, which would make me very sad. When I see someone suffering, I think of how to make everything all right. I keep doing it to the best of my ability, and I consider it the duty of every person. I understood one thing and that is—only education can help us rise above poverty and improve the future of our society and country. Perhaps my graduate and post-graduate educational institutions are the result of these thoughts.

It so happened that one day, I was going somewhere via Selaqui. On the way, I saw some children studying under a mulberry tree.

Some poor children from nearby areas were studying under that tree. I stopped and went to them. Their teacher stood up. When he saw me, he approached me. I kept looking at those children for a while. I felt sad that so many children spent their childhood in deprivation. So often, so many talented people are unable to make any progress due to these inadequacies. I asked, "Why are these children studying here under this tree? Don't they have any place to study?"

The teacher said, "Sir, we have not had classrooms for some time now. Earlier, Lalaji had a rice mill, in which I was given two rooms. I conducted classes in those two rooms. He was a very good man. But some time ago, he sold his rice mill. Those who bought it refused to allow me to teach children there. They wanted it for their use. Since then, I have been holding classes here. This is the only place we have right now." I felt very proud of that teacher because he was dedicated to the better future of those children.

But I could not bear to see those innocent children huddling under the shade of trees in the scorching sun. I thought of making some arrangements. I couldn't think of anything immediately. After running around for a couple of days, I came across a factory that was shut down. It had about six rooms available which could be used for the purpose. I bought those two *bighas* of land, had it cleaned, and converted it into a place for children to study. While arranging the place for the children to study, I remembered something that my friend Shri Hari Kishore Gaur had once told me. He had spoken to me about opening a school in my father's name. He said that since there was a college in my mother's name, I should at least open a school in my father's name. His words and making the arrangements for classes for these children sowed the idea of turning it into a school in my mind. I talked to the teacher about this, and he happily agreed. I did not cause any delay… I completed the government process required for opening the school and founded it in my father's name. I named it 'Pt Sureshanand Joshi Shishu Mandir'. So, there! I achieved this goal, too.

After some time, the classes had to be extended, so that also happened. In this way, the need to gradually extend the classes made it a centre for education up to higher secondary school.

I felt great that I could make some efforts for those poor kids. At the same time, I also felt proud that like I had done for my mother, I was also able to engrave my father's name on an educational institute.

So, this was about school, which I could have forgotten to write about… I remembered it at the right time.

Let us now go back to the point where we were talking about the 12 colleges that are affiliated with the university.

My younger brother Jagdish Joshi distributing sweets to the students in the school established in the name of our respected father

After continuously performing well in studies, sports, and other fields for three years after the establishment of the university, in 2013, an idea came to my mind that along with Law, Engineering and Management, some other subjects should also be started in the institutes. After consulting many experts, I felt that I should make the study of nature, medicine, and applied science available to the people through my university.

We confirmed our intent to start Bachelor of Pharmacy and Diploma in Pharmacy courses under Uttaranchal Institute of Pharmaceutical Sciences. I thought that if students were to gain knowledge in the field of medicine, we would be able to contribute significantly to the progress of society and the country. And thinking thus, I started working towards my goal.

I told my team to start working on all the standards as per the Pharmacy Council of India (PCI) and then applied to PCI. On the due date given by the Council, their team inspected all the standards and the Uttaranchal University received the accreditation by PCI.

I have spent my life in the midst of nature. That is why there is a special place for nature in my heart. I felt that by teaching children the skills of farming, I would be able to make some contribution to making Mother Earth green and fertile. So, with this thought, I geared up for the School of Agriculture to start courses in agriculture along with pharmacy courses. Its academic activities started in the year 2016.

At the time of starting these two new programmes, a thought flashed through my mind that if science was presented to children in the form of applied science, then my small effort to take our society and country to new heights would prove meaningful. It is said that necessity is the mother of invention, and science plays an important role in it. So, with this goal in mind, in the year 2016, I established the School of Applied Life and Sciences. Three years after becoming a university, we are now offering about 34 programs through six schools. I took great satisfaction in fulfilling my responsibilities towards our society and country.

You know that when a dreamer sees their dreams come true, it fills them with enthusiasm and boosts their morale. I did everything with full devotion and for the welfare of society. Perhaps this devotion played an important role in every success of mine.

I remember that I was watching the news on TV in 2017. I was very impressed with the art of reading and telling news. A thought crossed my mind that this skill can also be taught to children through the university and good and true journalism can also be promoted. With this thought, yet another thought came to my mind that my state Uttarakhand is a storehouse of scenic beauty. Around that time, I and my family had the privilege of travelling to different countries of the world including Dubai, London, Netherlands, Italy, Germany, Amsterdam, Belgium, Paris, Switzerland and Austria. I found that the people of Uttarakhand were especially involved in the hotel business and provided services in many cities of the world. Inspired by this, I thought that why not open a hotel management college in Uttarakhand for the hardworking people of the state and introduce this beauty to the world? With these thoughts, in 2018, the 'Uttaranchal School of Journalism and Mass Communication' and 'Uttaranchal School of Hotel and Hospitality Management' were established, where the nuances of media, hotels, and hospitality were taught to the students who were interested in this field.

After all these activities, you must have understood that I had started understanding every aspect of education very minutely. From the national to international level, I started providing international exposure to the students of my university by entering into bilateral agreements with other universities abroad for education, research and publication.

Apart from courses like technical knowledge, science, management, etc., I felt that every aspect of life should be shaped through education. With this thought, I established the 'School of Liberal Arts' in 2019 for subjects like literature, sociology, psychology and economics.

After establishing the 'School of Liberal Arts', I felt that we had touched every aspect that affected humanity. Everything was going well, and my university was also making gradual progress. On 27 January 2020, India's first case of COVID-19 was detected in Kerala. By the time we learnt about it, the disease had taken the form of an epidemic. The whole world was shaken. I shall tell you about this in the next chapter. First, let me tell you about my other colleges.

During the COVID pandemic, frontline warriors saved the lives of crores of people. Among them were the nursing staff who assisted the doctors and made significant contribution. Come to think of it, Mother Teresa herself is an embodiment of God, providing a unique example of service to every human being. Drawing inspiration from her, all the nurses serve with the same spirit of selflessness. Personally witnessing the role nurses played during COVID-19, when blood relatives refused to touch each other. Despite owning immense wealth, there were people for whom no one was willing to light the funeral pyres. It was during such a state of mind that I also thought of starting a nursing school through my university.

As I have already mentioned, every small incident can lead to a significant event. If you take care of small things, then big things also seem manageable. The small issue here was that I was thinking of opening a nursing college and the big issue was that opening a nursing college is challenging due to the standards mandated by the Indian Nursing Council (INC). Nonetheless, since I had decided to do it, I had no choice but to proceed. We began from scratch again, gathering resources such as buildings, teachers, labs, etc. First of all, I applied to the Uttarakhand Directorate of Medical Education. After receiving permission from them, I eagerly applied to the Indian Nursing Council. A date was fixed for the inspection to be carried out by INC. As soon as we received the recognition, the 'Uttaranchal College of Nursing' was established during the academic session of the year 2021-22. Along with its establishment, we also applied to get our university accredited by the best institution in the country. It is a very interesting story. Let me tell you.

Before I go ahead, I am happy to tell you that my university received 12 (B) recognition by UGC, which shows the prominence of our university in education, research, innovation and work done by us in social interests, etc. After receiving this recognition, our university has become eligible to receive all government grants given by UGC.

So, I was talking about how our university received NAAC A+ in January 2022.

And, today as I am writing this, the confidence in my hands and the way I am holding the pen is worth seeing. To be honest, as I am writing this, I cannot express the joy on my face that my university, which we started with one college at a time, is today the topmost university of Uttarakhand with NAAC A+ accreditation.

This honor was not easily attained. As mentioned earlier, understanding small things from a broader perspective and handling big tasks with ease were crucial. We worked tirelessly for two years, with my entire team putting in dedicated and continuous effort. Around 60 to 70 people from the university worked until 9 or 10 p.m. for a year, meticulously examining various documents to ensure accuracy. Subsequently, all these documents had to be uploaded on the NAAC portal. Over the past five years, my team had worked diligently in various areas such as research, sports, cultural programmes, placements, studies, patents or consultancy. My team had worked hard on all these things in the last 5 years. Yes, it is true that to upload the data of those 5 years together on the portal and ensure that whatever data we were putting there was correct, we used Excel. To be honest, all my faculty members performed every task with great honesty, the result of which was that we did not face any kind of problem while uploading the data. We uploaded that data at midnight and thanked God.

Here, I recall Dr N C Uniyal, whom we lost during the coronavirus crisis. We will always remember him and his work. The efficient manner in which he executed this task cannot be forgotten. Anyway, who can avoid what is destined? All task work was completed under his guidance. When the results came out, our university was the first university in Uttarakhand to get NAAC A+ accreditation. I would like to thank everyone who is reading my book and whoever contributed even a little because this is a huge achievement.

This happened at the beginning of January 2022. After that, when we sat together, we thought of opening two more new colleges. Today, everybody is talking about Artificial Intelligence, Machine Learning, Cloud Computing, etc. So, why not open a separate college for these branches? So, I established the 'Uttaranchal College of Computing Sciences', where we started providing computer science education. During the COVID pandemic, we saw many problems in the medical field. To overcome those problems, I thought of establishing a paramedical college, too. I hope that this college will definitely be able to make some contribution to the medical field in the country.

Keeping in mind the all-around progress of the university, which is based on research and innovation, Research Centres of Excellence were also established at Uttaranchal University. These centres conduct research on international topics like Industry 4.0 and Sustainable Development. These centres are dedicated to India's self-reliance and contribute to the country's missions like Make in India, Digital India, Swachh Bharat, etc.

We were thinking of opening another Health Sciences College at the university. We thought of making a small effort in the field of medicine for the country through Ayurvedic medicine and we started preparing for it. Today, as we send this book for publication, we have received approval to open an Ayurveda hospital, too.

So, this is a small story of our journey from a law college to the establishment of 13 colleges under Uttaranchal University.

❑

8

Corona Period and Our Courage

Before I move ahead, let me tell you a small story. A doctor, on the insistence of his 15-year-old son, took him to his hospital for a visit. But as soon as he reached the hospital, he received an emergency call for the operation of one of his patients, who had been in the ICU for several days. The father quickly got up, took his tools, stood with folded hands in front of the idol of God kept in the office for a while, and then left. His son was watching all of this.

His father came out of the operation theatre after about three hours and sat with the child.

The son asked, "What happened, father? Did that man survive?"

His father said, "Yes."

He could see from his father's face that everything was fine.

Then the son asked, "Father, why did you stand with folded hands in front of God while leaving?"

The father smiled and asked, "Why?"

The son said, "Please tell me!"

The father said, "I said to God, "Oh God! I may not understand your intentions, but I believe You will prevail. My only request is for You to assess that man's fate once – the decision to pass or fail is in Your hands. If there's anything You can do, please do it. His family depends on him. Until then, I will safeguard him. After that, You are free to do as You please.'"

I find this story very inspiring.

I don't know why, but I just recalled it.

Doctors are called the embodiment of God. This chapter will also tell you how it is so.

Today, I am writing this book, I am talking to you. But without God's grace, people's prayers, and the efforts of doctors, I would not have been sitting here. We had lost all hope.

I was also a victim of the catastrophe that had wreaked havoc across the world. Who does not remember that period of mayhem caused by COVID-19? Was there anyone who did not experience it? Even today, an ordinary cold, cough and fever cause one to be terrified.

I could have spoken about these things in the previous chapter. But I wanted to write about this agony separately. While the university was creating new records, this disaster opened a dark chapter for the entire world.

Let me start from the point where I suspected that a lockdown would be imposed in the country. Nobody knew anything about it. Scientists all over the world were shooting in the dark. The governments could not decide what to do. What would happen to the economy if a country with a population of more than 125 crores was closed down? What would happen to those families whose households run on daily wages? There were so many different rumours doing rounds. Some called it a ploy by the governments while others accused China. You must also be aware of what happened. You also must have gone through the difficult times. If you didn't face difficulties and overcame the havoc, be thankful to God, as everything happens according to His will.

Let's go back to the university which was waiting for me. We had meetings every day. Due to the lockdown, professors and employees at my university were anxious about their jobs. I could understand the situation of an ordinary family. What would happen to the families who entirely depended on the monthly salary? I assured everyone that none of the staff at my university would lose their jobs. I said that as long as I was there and as long as I had the capacity, every member of my university was a part of my family. Despite the lockdown, I promised to deliver the salaries of everyone from security guards and gardeners to deans and vice chancellors on the due date.

My mother used to say, "Son, the happiness that you get from bringing a smile to someone's face cannot be found anywhere else in the world. Whatever you do in life, be sure to be the reason for someone's smile. God will be with you."

It is said that everyone around you will support you during happy times. However, those who support us during difficult times are truly human. I am not highly educated, but I can decipher people's problems immediately. I am thankful to God that I have this power. When someone comes to my office, I understand what they want to say just by looking at them.

Ultimately, the expected happened. The government was forced to announce a lockdown in the country from 23 March 2020. Everything came to a standstill. A new challenge confronted everyone—to save their life, save their family, and earn a livelihood. Hardly anyone was untouched by this situation. Everyone faced challenges in some form or the other. That was the time when the importance of communication as an art came to the fore. People were locked in their homes, the streets were deserted, and everyone was glued to the TV or phone. Labourers across the country had started walking to their homes as if the birds were anxious to go to their nests. The catastrophic environment and difficult trials posed a challenge to all human beings to cope with the circumstances.

The coronavirus epidemic posed a challenge for Uttaranchal University as well. I did not lose courage because if the family head loses courage, the family becomes weak. I was already familiar with this experience because of my family and our struggles. Perhaps that is why the world considers fathers to be the toughest. I had already assured and promised my teachers and employees that no one would lose their jobs. By doing this, first of all, I put their worries to rest because I knew that only then would they be able to face the difficult situation with full courage. And then the university also owed its existence to them. We geared up to fight this challenge.

The duration of the lockdown kept getting extended. The government was also fighting with full force. The government remained vigilant, witnessing the devastating toll of the pandemic's global impact. I also took full responsibility for the students, teachers and employees in my colleges. The entire university was geared up to fight like warriors. While many private universities demanded a deduction in the salaries of their employees, I flatly refused to do so. I said, "I will not deduct the salary of any teacher or employee. The university has gained this position because of them. Their salaries will remain the same."

I started thinking about what I could do in this situation. During the lockdown, all the students left for their homes. I did not let their studies be affected. I prepared a complete strategy intending to help them complete their studies and examinations online. My son Abhishek supported me a lot in this task. Through ERP technology, classes for all children were conducted through desktops, laptops and mobiles. All necessary finances for this initiative were promptly secured, with no hesitation in allocating the required funds. We successfully implemented this during the lockdown, ensuring that the academic year for the children remained productive. Every step was taken in adherence to regulations and deadlines, with meticulous care provided to the students. This accomplishment was made possible by the dedicated support of my resilient team, who stood by me in every situation.

During the COVID pandemic, everyone saw how labourers across the country were forced to migrate to their hometowns. Some people found the modes of transport while some did not. Some people travelled by bicycle while some had to walk. In that situation, how could I leave the labourers working in my college on their own? Even if they were not directly connected with me, I felt equally responsible for their lives. I did as much as I could. I made arrangements for all the labourers who were engaged in the construction work of the university—right from their living arrangements to rations, food packets, medicines, etc.

Beyond the confines of the university, I endeavored to extend assistance to the wider community to the best of my capacity. Food packets were also arranged on a daily basis for labourers and the needy through the Dehradun Police.

You can gauge the food's quality by the simple fact that I shared in the same provisions.

I believed that whether it was in my power to eliminate this darkness or not, I must steadfastly continue illuminating the lamp of aid. Failing to do so would be a weight I couldn't bear.

Grateful for the abundance given by God, I recalled a couplet:

Desh hamein deta hai sabkuch
Hum bhi to kuch dena seekhein

(The country gives us so much

We should also give something in return.)

I loved these lines, but now it was time to live these lines. While acknowledging my limitations in effecting significant change, I committed to contributing in the most meaningful way possible. I contributed Rs 11 lakh to the Chief Minister's Relief Fund. Apart from this, the teachers and non-teaching staff of my university donated a part of their salary to ensure their participation in this noble mission.

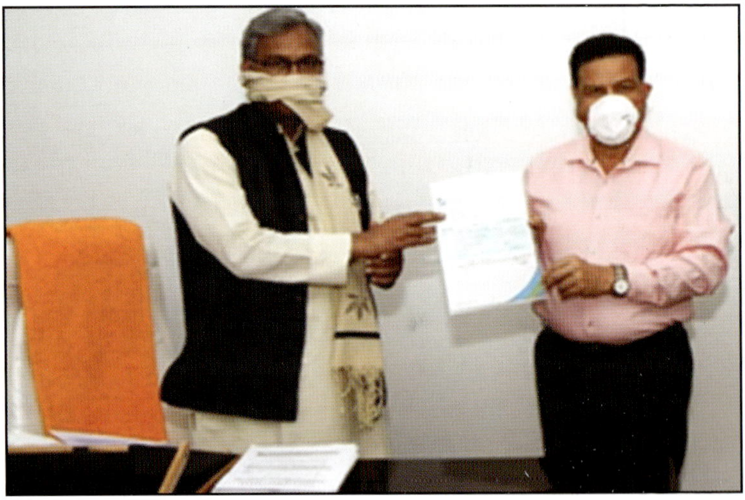

On behalf of the Uttaranchal University family, handing over the assistance amount to Chief Minister Shri Trivendra Singh Rawatji during the Covid period

I treated the university like a family. This family also supported me very well. We continued to fight together, and gradually everything was fine. Gradually, the lockdown was lifted across the country, and people started going back to work. But no one knew that worse was yet to come. The impending arrival of the second wave of the coronavirus was poised to inflict even greater devastation on the country. This wave ruined many families. It took away many family members, leaving families distraught. As I pen down these words, an eerie chill runs down my spine, vividly bringing forth the harrowing scenes playing out before my eyes.

The second wave was a big challenge for everyone—whether poor or rich. The news that was shown throughout the day was heart-wrenching. I stopped watching the news. But even if I closed my eyes what was going to change? When you close your eyes, you may not be able to see the world. But it does not mean that it has ceased to exist.

Then one day, I felt a little feverish. I understood what it could be. When the fever rose, I underwent a corona test. The report was positive. My wife Anu was also infected with corona. But by the grace of God, she was cured. But my infection was severe. I was nervous, which made it even worse. My oxygen level had also dropped. My family got me admitted to Max Hospital. I shudder at the mere memory of it.

That scene in the hospital and deaths on the mass level... I am at a loss as to how to describe that scene... Only a writer can express that in words... I cannot do it. God forbid, it's a sight one wouldn't wish even upon an enemy.

Amidst the ordeal, I drew strength from within, reminding myself that I had caused no harm. I held onto the belief that

God would assist us. The corona ward—where you had no acquaintances, no family member was allowed to meet you—you saw people die right in front of your eyes, and you could not help even if you wanted to. Everywhere, you could see people suffering. No one there knew whether they would wake up the next morning.

My body had become weak. But till now in my life, I had never accepted defeat; so, I was not going to accept defeat at this point either. I prepared myself that I would face whatever was in store for me. At the worst, I would die. What else could happen? Nobody here is immortal!

I would get to know through the phone that people were praying for me. They said, "You will definitely recover. We are all waiting for you. God is with you." This kept me going. This is what I have earned to date. Even if something were to happen, I was not afraid. But prayers, doctors' efforts, and God's grace paid off. I recovered and returned home.

I cannot even describe all that I saw… I saw a number of people die on the bed right next to me while I was there. Well, I think we should leave this topic here. I cannot write any further. It was a dreadfully dark period. I just want to thank all those nurses and doctors who risked their lives attending to every patient.

Amidst the hardship, a silver lining emerged, which I want to share with you. It so happened that some young men were also admitted to my ward. They were losing patience out of frustration and their oxygen level was also dropping continuously. I would keep talking to them and encourage them. They were younger than me. When I received food from my home, I would offer them. Initially, they would hesitate. But when they recovered a little, they would also ask me to get things of their choice. After I left the hospital by the grace of God and the prayers of people, I still kept in touch with them. The best part is that even today they call me and enquire about my wellbeing. It is said that the strength of relationships is boundless. We should always do our best to maintain relationships.

I will share some more fresh memories with you in the next chapter...

❑

9

My Beloved *Boi*

Dikha jo thoda dukhi wo
Aankh bharke roi hogi,
Main na soya rat main to
Nahi wo bhi soi hogi
Wo duaa, jiski bodolat
Yeh unchai chhu raha hoon,
Yeh wahan se aai hogi
Jahan meri boi hogi.

Do you know who *Boi* is?

Well, even if you did not know this yet, these lines must have reminded you of your mother. Yes, *Boi* means mother. If you are from the hilly region, then you would know that a mother is called *Boi*.

This is the last chapter of this book from me. After this, I have nothing left to say about myself. I have captured as much of my journey, of 62 years, as I could from my memory in these few pages. Now, this is the last chapter.

Allow me to commence this chapter by recounting the day when Mr. Mukesh Dhasmana, the director of Garhwali films, visited my office. He lived in Mumbai. He is also a good friend of mine. I offered him tea and we chatted about work and life in general. Then he narrated a script to me—it was a very poignant story. My heart ached, and there were tears in my eyes. I felt angry and immensely sad at the same time. Let me tell you what gave rise to these feelings in me. First, I will tell you why I felt sad.

Basically, that story was based on the sacrifice of a *Boi,* i.e., mother. It was about how a mother brings up her son even in the face of hardships and makes him capable. This story reminded me of my mother. I became emotional. Subsequently, I shared my mother's story with them, eliciting a compassionate reaction. He, moved by the narrative, entrusted me with the responsibility of producing his film. I readily agreed because in this era of vulgar films, being involved in such a subject was an important decision; it was like sending a beautiful message to society.

Abhishek Tower was chosen for the selection of supporting actors in the film because that was the starting point of education for us. And, of course, as a film producer, I wanted to start from there.

It was a little difficult to find artists for the film. It was not as if there were no artists here. But they were uncomfortable in front of the camera since they lacked experience. Additionally, the film being in the Garhwali dialect presented difficulties, as clear pronunciation and command of the language proved challenging for the artists. However, every artist immersed themselves in their craft, living a life akin to the characters they portrayed.

As mentioned earlier, Mukesh Dhasmanaji had written the script of the film. Now, we needed songs for the film, and since the film was about a mother, the songs of the film also needed to meet a certain standard. Well, everyone thought of only one name— Jeet Singh Negiji, who was a famous Garhwali lyricist. Today he is no more, but many of his songs are still remembered. Mukeshji decided that Negiji would write the songs for this film. He wrote the songs as well as dialogues for *Meri Pyaari Boi*. Folk singer Santosh Khetwalji sang those songs. We all met Negiji and narrated the story to him. He loved the story and agreed to write for it. Many songs of this film became quite popular on YouTube.

I had no idea what happens during the making of a film. But then Dhasmanaji was there. He took care of everything. I was always there when I was needed and left no stone unturned. The work started after everything was decided, such as—where the film would be shot, on which days it would be shot, and which artists would shoot on which day. Mukeshji said that they needed a house for the film where they could shoot some parts. I wondered which house it could be where the shooting could take place. After thinking for a while, I offered the use of my house. We shifted all the stuff into two rooms in the house. The subject of this film compelled me to do all this because I really liked it, and my mother was always in my heart.

As I've mentioned previously, my approach to everything is wholehearted, with a readiness to contribute to its success— an ethos instilled by my mother. I remained deeply involved in the film, and with gratitude for God's grace, college admissions progressed smoothly, bringing me joy. As you now understand, I never shied away from opportunities but embraced them wholeheartedly.

The entire team worked hard, and the film was completed. When the shooting was going on, whenever I had free time from college, I would go and watch the shooting. I would sit there for a while and then take my leave.

I remember an incident. It was the day of Holi. That day, a song was being shot, in which about 20 actors were participating. That song also became very popular. While going for the shooting, I took with me a basket of *gujhiya*. Thus, we also celebrated Holi with all the artists.

This marked the conclusion of the shooting phase. After the film was completed, we began the preparations for its release. Wherever there was a need for something, I always tried to ensure that its quality did not diminish in any way.

Now you might be thinking—we know that it was a film based on a mother's struggle. But what was its story?

Well, allow me to swiftly share the poignant story with you.

The story goes like this. A widowed mother works in other people's houses, fields, etc., to build a good future for her son Suraj. She spends all the money she earns from her work on her son's education, food, etc. She just spends enough on herself to survive. The mother thinks that when her son grows up, she will be rid of all her troubles. With these thoughts, she works twice as hard and saves money. When her son grows up, she invests all her savings in getting him admitted to a good college in Dehradun.

As it often happens with youthful hearts, a parallel unfolds in this narrative. Suraj ventures to the city and falls deeply in love with Neelam. After several years of courtship, he marries her without a word to his mother, leaving her in prolonged anticipation. These moments evoke profound sadness in me—how can a child subject his mother to such prolonged waiting?

Nevertheless, the tale moves forward, and my conversations invariably circle back to my mother.

When the mother learns that her son has married, she feels hurt. However, she does not express this pain to her son. Instead, she happily says to him, “Son, bring our daughter-in-law here. At least let me observe some rituals with her.”

On her insistence, Suraj brings his wife to their house in the village. The mother is very happy. She also invites the villagers for a meal to share this happiness. She welcomes her daughter-in-law. She also asks her son to stay with her in the village and carry on with his job from there. Listening to his mother, the son decides to stay back. But his wife does not like the atmosphere in the village. She voices complaints about the inconveniences posed by the presence of cattle dung, the responsibility of caring for his mother, and the overall lack of material comforts in the village.

She always grumbles to her husband about the deficiencies of the village. One day, the widowed mother’s son and daughter-in-law talk about going to the city for a while. They leave but never return. The mother, waiting for them for several days, eventually passes away, her last breath drawn in anticipation of her child's return.

As I write this, I have tears in my eyes. I do not have enough courage to write about it further. But I would definitely say that every child should respect their mother. As I said in the beginning, I was also angry. It was because the child did not take care of his mother. He left his mother to suffer alone because of his wife. In this emotional story, we must appreciate Mukesh Dhasmana Ji's remarkable storytelling skills. Crafting such a universally touching tale is praiseworthy. This emotional journey requires not only good writing but also talented actors. Hence, we carefully chose actors for the key roles.

In this way, many actors contributed to making the film brilliant with their excellent acting. The film's success lies in its ability to reflect the poignant essence of the story.

This film always reminds me of my mother. I can see her struggle for her children very clearly in this film. I was glad that I was a part of this film.

By the way, I also played a small role in this film. This opportunity arose suddenly. One day, Mukeshji came and said to me, "Joshi Ji, there is a very small role of a doctor in the film. Will you play it?"

I was game for it. I said that I would definitely play it. So, I also ended up playing a small role in the film. Do watch the film!

Playing the role of a doctor for the film 'Meri Pyari Boi'

The name of this film was *Meri Pyaari Boi* (My Beloved Mother).

I should have mentioned the film earlier since it was a long time ago. It happened around the year 2002-03. However, I wanted to talk about it at the end. Two reasons guided this decision. Firstly, as everyone's world originates from their mother's world, concluding my book with a tribute to my mother seemed only fitting. The journey began with my childhood, encompassing her world, and so it concludes.

Secondly, film is an art form, and ending our conversation on this note seemed apropos.

So, this was my journey. I haven't stopped yet and I won't stop as long as I have the energy.

I don't know how you felt as you travelled with me till here. But I am very sad as I stop this book here. This was my job for several months. I used to think—today I will talk about this, I will write about that. Now it is complete. But I am happy that I was able to express myself through words. Maybe you can learn something from my experience. That will be my success.

I am not saying that you should do the same things that I did because times and circumstances would be different. I became successful by doing certain things. But it is not necessary that you also become successful by doing the same things in the same way. The challenges differ according to the times and so does the way of confronting them. Nevertheless, some things will always help you, which you will always need in order to be successful. I am talking about four points which I have gleaned from my experience.

First: Continue to learn.

Second: Never miss an opportunity.

Third: Do not lose courage.

Fourth: Always respect your parents.

These four elements will change your life. That's all I wanted to say. Now, I will take your leave.

Stay happy, have fun, stay busy, and keep moving forward.

Me with my wife Anu and my children- Abhishek and Ankita

Unforgettable Moments with Incomparable People

Courtesy meeting with Her Excellency the Honorable President Smt. Draupadi Murmuji at Rashtrapati Bhavan, New Delhi.

Courtesy meeting with Honorable Governor of Uttarakhand, Lieutenant General (Retired) Gurmeet Singhji at Raj Bhavan, Dehradun

Courtesy meeting with Honorable Chief Minister Uttarakhand, Shri Pushkar Singh Dhamiji

Courtesy meeting with Honorable Padmavibhushan Shri Amitabh Bachchanji at his bungalow Jalsa

Courtesy meeting with Honorable Governor of Maharashtra, Shri Bhagat Singh Koshyariji at Raj Bhavan, Maharashtra

Honorable Governor, Uttarakhand, Shri Sudarshan Agarwalji

Presenting a memento to Honorable Governor of Uttarakhand, Shri Aziz Qureshi during the Blood Donation Camp program organized at Uttaranchal University

Offering holy Ganga water of Gangottaridham to ISRO Chairman Shri S. Somnath during the program 'Akash Tattva' organized at Uttaranchal University.

Honorable Governor Shri Surjit Singh Barnala during the inauguration of the new campus of Law College, Dehradun

Presenting a bouquet to Dr. Jitender Singh, the special guest of Akash Tattva, a program organized at Uttaranchal University, Minister of State with Independent Charge of Science and Technology, Department of Earth Sciences, Atomic Energy, Space Sciences, Prime Minister's Office, Government of India

During the program Akash Tattva organized at Uttaranchal University

During the 'A Talk from an Expert' program organized at Uttaranchal University, with renowned defense analyst Major General (Retd.) G.D. Bakshiji

During the Teacher's Day program organized at Law College, Dehradun, with former Lok Sabha Speaker and MP Shri P.A. Sangamaji

Honorable Minister Shri Ramesh Pokhriyal "Nishank" and Suryakant Dhasma Nazi in happy mood at an event organized at Law College, Dehradun

'A talk from an expert' organized at Uttaranchal University

10

Our Father

Hello, readers!

This book has reached its completion at my father's end, spanning nine chapters that document his entire life. Now, my sister Ankita and I, Abhishek, are collaborating to prepare its tenth chapter. Initially, the book was intended to consist only of these nine chapters, and our awareness of its existence surfaced only upon its completion. We discovered that our father, the best in the world, had been working on this project when he handed us the finished book.

While we were well-acquainted with our father's struggles, courage, and love for us, his hidden talent as a writer came as a surprise. During our family dinners, where numerous topics were discussed, the book was never mentioned. Ankita and I have been actively involved in supporting our father with his university work as a brother-sister duo. Growing up, we perceived our father as well-established, but his past was rarely explored in our conversations, limited to the names and village of our grandparents. We did not get to spend much time with our grandmother, but we spent around 10-12 years with our grandfather. He may have mentioned it at some point, but given our age, we may not have paid much attention. We also got to know our father through this book when he called both of us and handed it to us to get it published.

Now it seems that we did see that our father had been writing something for a long time. But we could never figure out what he was writing. This came to light the day Papa called Ankita and I to his office at the university, which was after 5 p.m. when the university usually closes and the staff goes home. So, both of us went to see him. Papa talked to us a little. I admire one habit of my father very much. I can say that I have never seen him get upset under any circumstances. No one can take away his smile because he is not dependent on any materialistic thing. Papa asked in the same manner, “How are you? All well? What did you do today?” Both of us took turns to share a few things with him.

Papa talked like this for a while. Then he suddenly took out a diary along with some pages from his cupboard and placed them in front of both of us.

We looked at it. As we opened it, we asked, “What is this, Papa?”

Then my father said, “Children, I have written this about myself. It is about my journey from childhood till now. I just felt that something like this should be done. So, I started writing it. As it stands now, it is complete from my side. I hope that you will get it published. Now, I have no idea how it can be done. I hand over this responsibility to you.”

We opened it a little, read a couple of pages, and then looked at each other. Then we decided to take it home to read. To be honest, we also wanted to get to know our father better. Now that he had written it, nothing could be better. We read it for about three to four days, going back and forth. Then we organised it by sequencing the content. We talked to Shravan Kumarji, one of our staff members. Through him, we were introduced to poets Sandeep Dwivediji and Shraddha Vajpayeeji, and we talked to them about the book. We talked about organising the book from the point of view of publishing it.

We had heard Dr Shravan Kumar reciting poetry many times. We also knew that 25 of his own books had been published by various publishers. So, we told him we wanted to get this autobiography published by a good publisher. He thought for about 15-20 days and then selected 'Prabhat Prakashan', which is India's best Hindi publishing house. He also told us that this publication has published autobiographies and biographies of leading personalities such as Kalam Sahab, Modiji, Yogiji and almost all the leaders of India.

While doing all this, my sister Ankita had an idea. Dr Anil Dixitji, a staff member of our university, was writing something like a biography about our father. He has also written the university's anthem. In his book, he shared the thoughts and experiences of many people about Papa.

We thought, why not add a chapter to include memorable experiences that people had with my father? We immediately started working on this idea and agreed that until the book was published, Papa should not know anything about this. We decided amongst ourselves, and thus, this chapter was added to the autobiography of my father on behalf of me and my sister.

Since Papa had assigned this task to us, we had to accomplish it with full responsibility. We included some more experiences along with those included in that biography. So, here is this additional chapter written by both of us. In this, the love of the people for our father has been put together.

We first met Dharam Singh Nakotiji, who is a close friend of our father. We asked him about our father.

He said, “I remember the time when Jitender Joshi’s factory was about to close down. It seems as if it all happened just yesterday. He was a little sad. But even at that time, you could see confidence in his eyes. Based on my experience, I advised him that since the real estate business was flourishing those days, a hardworking and honest person like him could make unprecedented progress if he joined it. I am happy that within a few days his simplicity, honesty, and hard work paid off, and he stood at the forefront of the real estate business in the state.”

We enjoyed hearing about Papa’s passion from his dear friend.

After this, we talked with Akash Panwarji. Papa used to often mention him. Panwarji had also started the real estate business at the same time as Papa. He spoke with great pleasure about our father, “Both of us had started the same business. I am still continuing in the same business. But Jitenderji travelled extensively and achieved many successes. From the very beginning, he was a very courageous person, and he was also very practical. He neither did anything hastily nor late. Once he decided to do something, he would do it, and he did it on time. This was his special quality.”

Now I am remembering Satyendra Sajwanji. Papa often speaks about him. My grandfather’s entire family lived in his house on rent. That means, some years of my father's childhood were spent in his house. We could not meet him. But my father says that he respected our family a lot. He had great affection for my entire family. He would often pull my father's leg and say, "Barrister Saheb, where are you going?" If I ever meet Sajwanji, I will definitely ask him about Papa.

Now we remember Ajab Lalji—my father's friend. They also worked together on many occasions. Recently Papa also went to meet him. We feel good and inspired when Papa remembers everyone despite his busy schedule and talks to us about those things.

Then when we mention our father, we remember Govind Prasad Sharmaji. Papa keeps telling us that it was Sharmaji who had inspired him to start the law college. He had also said, "Start the college. Let me know wherever you need me. I am always with you. I have full confidence that whatever you do, you will give your best." Papa tells us that Sharmaji boosted his morale significantly; otherwise, opening a law college was a completely new task, a new challenge for Papa.

Papa also recalls Hari Kishore Gaurji, a friend in the real estate business with whom he worked many years ago. Papa credits Gaurji for suggesting the idea of opening a school for poor children. Gaurji had said, "Jitender ji, you have done good work in the name of your mother—you opened a college and formed a trust. Now, you should do something in your father's name, too. You can even open a school." Inspired by this, Papa founded a school in the name of our grandfather Pandit Sureshanand Joshi, where free education is given to poor and economically backward children. My dad often mentions Gaurji in discussions.

Shri Hemchand Devraniji, the adviser of Uttaranchal University, who is my mother's cousin, says, "Jitender Joshi is a personality in himself. He never compares himself or his work with anyone. He always says that one should not get involved in comparisons because there is no end to it. Once you get involved in comparisons, pride or disappointment starts creeping inside you. Then the joy and affinity within you die. He jokingly says that hope and faith are never wrong. It simply depends on us whom we hope from and whom we believe. Although every person believes himself to be a king, the circumstances are visible to the one who listens and tolerates them." Devraniji is a scholar and distinguished administrative officer in his own right. He also believes that the road of desires is long, but by thinking better, we take the road as per our needs.

And finally, we met Dr Rajesh Bahugunaji and talked to him about our father. He said, "My first meeting with Bhaiji (Shri Jitender Joshi Ji) took place around the year 2000. The topic of our discussion was the establishment of a law college, for which he had great enthusiasm. That was the time when there was not a single law college offering a five-year LLB course in Uttarakhand and its surrounding areas. I was stunned at Joshi Ji's passion. I saw that a person associated with real estate was so eager to enter the world of education that he was ready to work day and night for it. When I got the opportunity to work closely with Joshi Ji about 18 months before the establishment of Law College, Dehradun, I found that I was working with a person who not only dreamt of earning money but was also eager to do something for society, which the next generations will be proud of. During this time, I was so impressed by his thought process, simplicity, working style, ambition, and that he walked towards his goal with the confidence of certain success that I left my job in the government department and decided to join Joshi Ji. I am proud that in this journey of 20-22 years, I have had the opportunity to remain his close associate from the first day till he wrote his autobiography."

Thus, there are many people whom we know through our father and many people whom we know personally, who have been his guides and well-wishers. Even today, everyone has immense love for Papa.

It is a moment of tremendous pride for a son and daughter to hear about their father's achievements from other people and to see their father receiving so much love from everyone. He inspires them to raise his honour higher, to make him feel proud of them, and to accomplish something new and great like him.

With gratitude,

Abhishek and Ankita

About the Translator

Dr. Kumar Shravan is by heart a Hindi Poet, by passion a Writer, and by profession a Professor of Communication. Dr Kumar is a Professor & Dean of School of Liberal Arts & Dean Student Welfare and additional responsibility of Incharge, International Affairs, Uttaranchal University. 27 books are in his credit published by Cambridge University Press, UK, and Atlantic Publishers, India. 28 Research Papers, 11 Patents and 03 Copyrights position his innovative and creative approach very firmly. He is also carrying the responsibility of National Vice-Presidentship of the English Language Teachers' Association of India. He has also received the Teacher Excellence Award by UGC in 2020. He has delivered more than 135+ lectures as Plenary Speaker/ Resource Person in National and International Seminars, Conferences, Workshops, and Webinars. He has organised more than 50 International academic and more than 350+ extracurricular mega events.

❑